DAVENPORT'S MICHIGAN WILLS AND ESTATE PLANNING LEGAL FORMS

Alexander William Russell

Ernest Charles Hope

Second Edition – 2015

Published by Davenport Press

ALSO PUBLISHED BY DAVENPORT PRESS

Davenport's Florida Wills And Estate Planning Legal Forms
Davenport's Georgia Wills And Estate Planning Legal Forms
Davenport's Illinois Wills And Estate Planning Legal Forms
Davenport's Indiana Wills And Estate Planning Legal Forms
Davenport's Maryland Wills And Estate Planning Legal Forms
Davenport's Massachusetts Wills And Estate Planning Legal Forms
Davenport's Minnesota Wills And Estate Planning Legal Forms
Davenport's Missouri Wills And Estate Planning Legal Forms
Davenport's Nebraska Wills And Estate Planning Legal Forms
Davenport's New Jersey Wills And Estate Planning Legal Forms
Davenport's New York Wills And Estate Planning Legal Forms
Davenport's North Carolina Wills And Estate Planning Legal Forms
Davenport's Ohio Wills And Estate Planning Legal Forms
Davenport's Pennsylvania Will And Estate Planning Legal Forms
Davenport's Tennessee Wills And Estate Planning Legal Forms
Davenport's Texas Wills And Estate Planning Legal Forms
Davenport's Wyoming Wills And Estate Planning Legal Forms

Booklet Series

Davenport's California Will And Estate Planning Legal Forms Booklet
Davenport's Maine Will And Estate Planning Legal Forms Booklet
Davenport's Wisconsin Will And Estate Planning Legal Forms Booklet

Accounting C.P.A. Series

Davenport's Federal Estate And Gift Tax 2015 Basic Forms Review
Davenport's Spreadsheet And Print Templates For 1099-MISC 2015

COPYRIGHT © 2015 BY ALEX W. RUSSELL

Publication Description:
Davenport's Michigan Wills And Estate Planning Legal Forms;
Second Edition; 2015;
Authored by Alexander William Russell and Ernest Charles Hope;
Published by **DAVENPORT PRESS** 54 Amelia Avenue, West St. Paul, MN 55118

TABLE OF CONTENTS

CHAPTER 1
GUIDE TO BOOK AND FORMS

BOOK HAS 10 FORMS BUT MOST PEOPLE ONLY USE A FEW FORMS

In this book 10 legal forms are provided but most people only use a few forms, and the forms are:

Form 1. Michigan Statutory Will (a "Will" is a legal document that lets people control issues after their death, and the "Statutory Will" form is written by the Michigan legislature to help most people and it is well accepted by judges but it has some inflexible language about gifting and favors family);

Form 2. Last Will And Testament (With Guardians) (this Will form uses flexible language to let people gift their property and money as wanted, and this form also has a "Guardians" paragraph to in case it is needed name guardians to care for persons under 18 and their property);

Form 3. Last Will And Testament (No Guardians) (this is a Will form like Form 2 but with no paragraph on guardians and is for people with no child under 18 and not giving anything to minors);

Form 4. Self-Proving Affidavit (this form is often done with a Will to help the later process after a death of proving a Will was signed correctly, and the form also makes it more likely a Will is followed);

Form 5. Tangible Personal Property List (lets people write down in lists outside a Will wanted gifts to occur on death of "tangible personal property" like clothes, furniture, vehicles, and jewelry);

Form 6. Codicil (this form can make changes to an existing Will, but most just do a new Will);

Form 7. Durable Power of Attorney for Health Care (in case a person is later incapacitated and unable to control their own health care this form lets a person name a "Patient Advocate" to control health care (often this is a spouse, adult child, or friend), and also if wanted give health care orders);

Form 8. Do-Not-Resuscitate Order (this form lets a person say paramedics and other medical personnel should not try to restart the heart or breathing (usually this care is called C.P.R.));

Form 9. Durable General Power of Attorney (this form lets power over a person's money, property, and more be shared with someone like spouse or trusted friend to let them do things); and

Form 10. Power Of Attorney Over Child (this form lets a parent give power over a child so if a child is away from parents someone else can make decisions, like with medical or school issues).

1

BOOK'S FOCUS IS MICHIGAN WILLS AND ESTATE PLANNING LAW AND FORMS

This book provides in one convenient place a review of some Michigan law and a good range of ready to use Michigan legal forms. This book's focus is Wills and Estate Planning which deals with how a person can act now to control on illness or death their health care, property, money, children, and other matters. Michigan law applies if people live here more than temporarily. To help people this book is short and quickly shows legal forms, and people who want can easily get more information. This book does go into many details and has many forms that some people may want to skip.

DOWNLOAD OR PHOTOCOPY FORMS, WITH CHANGES RARELY NEEDED

To get copies of this book's forms to use people can 1) download forms free as Appendix A shows, or 2) photocopy pages from this book. Book pages that are forms don't have bottom page numbers. When filling out forms people can use a computer to add words or just handwrite in words, but legally people should handwrite signatures and nearby dates in permanent pen or marker. Most forms show with underlining where words, signatures, and dates should be added (like, "I name _____ as agent"). This book's writing also shows several ways to add legal language or change words in forms, but these bigger changes are rarely needed and can by risky and are not recommended.

BOOK AND FORMS SHOULD BE SUFFICIENT IF ONE HAS USUAL SITUATION

This book and its forms cannot cover everything but should be sufficient for people with usual situations and wishes. Wills and Estate Planning forms actually do simple things most people can understand and can do for themselves. This book quickly explains many legal areas to help show often no special action is needed. Half this book's forms are not even really written by a lawyer but are standard forms (many with instructions or written to be self-explanatory) done by the state legislature, by a state agency, or they just have basic words to match a clear state law.

PEOPLE WITH UNUSUAL SITUATIONS OR WISHES MAY NEED A LAWYER

People with unusual situations or wishes may need a lawyer for Wills and Estate Planning like those with: 1) wealth over $5 million, 2) complex family situations, 3) unusual wishes for gifts, or 4) big family medical concerns (like person with long-term care or special needs). But using a lawyer can take many visits over months, cost $1000-$3000 a person, and results vary (and many forms are redone every 3-5 years raising costs ten-fold over a lifetime). In life people often must weigh the likely costs and benefits and decide if to pay lawyers, and most don't use lawyers for Wills and similar forms. Often Wills and Estate Planning documents are not vital but later save others small costs, or problems are avoided by basic words any form has without need for fancy lawyer writing, or documents are never used or not used for decades. But wealthier or older people want find a lawyer more worthwhile. Many people wish lawyers cost less and used simpler options. In general people also often don't use lawyers even for bigger things (when maybe they should) like home or car buying, jobs, accidents, loans, financial planning, and family issues. **This book and forms are not a substitute for legal advice and do not create any lawyer-client relationship.**

SOME DOCUMENTS NOT IN THIS BOOK ARE LESS COMMONLY USED

Some documents people may have heard of are less commonly used and are not in this book.

Property, debt, and password lists are informally written by many people yearly to help family and others sort out things after their death.

"Revocable Living Trust" papers may be suggested to transfer item by item most things into a trust for years, mainly so maybe property transfers faster after a death and to avoid small costs and probate work for others, but this is rare and can be costly and make living and paperwork difficult for years.

"Childrens Trust" papers to have a trust hold a minor's property after a death may be suggested, but a Will already names a "conservator" to manage and spend a minor's property and money on them until 18, and trusts mainly are done to avoid small costs of yearly court review that helps avoid misuse.

"Organ Donation" forms are often done in state ID or drivers license forms (this is easiest), or through Secretary of State offices or STATE.SOS.MI.US or 1-800-482-4881. State law also says family can consent to organ donation at death and cannot block any donation already arranged.

For funerals and burials in Michigan closest family (like spouse or child) control this no matter what is written but some people still put requests in written forms, but usually for funeral and burial issues people just talk to family and maybe make arrangements with funeral homes and cemeteries.

3

CHAPTER 2
BASIC TERMS AND LAW

SOME IDEAS AND WORDS ARE BASIC TO WILLS AND ESTATE PLANNING

Some ideas and words are basic to Wills and Estate Planning law and forms.

■ <u>A person who has died is called a "decedent"</u> or "deceased".

■ A "Will" is a document often done by a person to control some issues after their death. A "Will" is often called "Last Will And Testament" and anyone doing a Will is called "Testator".

■ "Property" is anything of value and is either 1) "real property" which is land, buildings, and fixtures attached to the land, or 2) "personal property" which is any other property like money, accounts, jewelry, house furnishings, appliances, equipment, and vehicles.

■ A "beneficiary" is a person getting things without fully paying, like from a gift in a Will.

■ "Heir" is a person who gets property on a death due to a Will or state law (they "inherit").

■ "Probate" is a legal process that may help with issues after a person's death, and it can help transfer property, pick guardians, show everyone things are done fairly, handle creditors, and more. Michigan probate unlike some states is fairly fast and affordable and also has simpler options.

■ An "Executor" (now officially called a "Personal Representative") is the person in charge of a probate process and other things after a death, and often is a spouse, adult child, or friend.

■ "Notary" (also called a "notary public") is a person approved by the state to be involved and make signing of certain documents more official, and they can be found at banks, insurance agents, court, or (often best to avoid delay and bother) can be hired from the phonebook. Signing "under seal" is a more official way to sign, and is done by signing by an official seal or the word "SEAL". The word "respectively" just means "in the order just said" and often is used to refer to a list of names.

■ Michigan laws are "statutes" and are grouped in "chapters" and big parts are called a "code". State laws are all in the "Michigan Compiled Laws" at legislature.mi.gov, and references in books can look like "MCL 202.1" or similar. Some law books have "annotation" notes. Laws about Wills and persons needing protection are in the "Estates and Protected Individuals Code" or "EPIC" starting at MCL 700.1101. Court rules may apply. Federal law is the U.S. Code.

■ Wills and similar usually involve the local "Probate Court" rather than bigger "Circuit Court" or smaller "District Court". Wills for safekeeping can filed early at court but withdrawn if ever wanted.

4

"ESTATE" MEANS PROPERTY OF DECEDENT OR BODY MANAGING THINGS

Property of a decedent that on death did not transfer automatically to other owners is called the "estate" of decedent, or the "probate estate". After a death there may also be an "estate" body run by an executor to do things and temporarily hold property, and a decedent's accounts and other property might be renamed for a few months like "Estate of [decedent]".

"NON-PROBATE PROPERTY" TRANSFERS IGNORE ANY WILL

Importantly, property that for some reason automatically transfers on a death to other owners is called "non-probate property" and such property transfers as arranged even if a Will names the property. Examples are a) "beneficiary" forms name someone to get accounts or other things, b) property is held by 2 people as "joint tenants", c) life insurance names a person as beneficiary, d) an "enhanced life estate deed" naming another person is put in land records, and e) transfer-on-death or pay-on-death accounts are used. Arranging non-probate transfers is called "avoiding probate" if done for most things, but it is rare since it can make living and paperwork difficult for many years just to save others small work and costs. When doing a Will people should consider non-probate transfers that may occur.

OWNERSHIP OF PROPERTY DETERMINES WHAT CAN BE GIFTED

A person can only gift by Will or other way property and money they own, and many rules affect this.

Very basically, in Michigan a person usually owns all they earn, and also owns things or parts of things their resources contribute the funds to get or improve.

Michigan is not a "community property" state (like California or Texas) where a spouse owns half a spouse's income and gains (but things from when living in such states often remains owned 50/50).

People can anytime change owners by doing an agreement, gifting, or failing to keep track of things.

For property with title documents (real estate or vehicles) or where people list owners (like accounts) listed persons are owners unless people can prove a mistake, an agreement to share or return, or they worked or gave resources to get or improve things not as a gift and legally they should own a share.

There are many ways several can own the same property, but often people are "tenants in common" with a 50% or other share they can sell, gift, or Will and which doesn't go to other owners on death.

A person in life is free to make gifts or sell property even property named in a Will, and family often say a person verbally gave them some needed things (so gifts of these a Will should not be followed).

Basically, people doing a Will should ask questions and see what they own and can give.

REAL ESTATE IS OWNED AS TITLE PAPERS SAY WHICH CAN LIMIT GIFTING

Real estate is usually owned however title papers say, which can affect gifting:

a) normal or "separate" ownership usually occurs if just 1 person is listed on title, then the owner usually has power to sell or gift during life and to gift by Will;

b) "tenants in common" may occur if several are listed on title, then an owner has a percent share (like 50%) they can sell or gift in life or gift by Will (this is common way of owning many things);

c) "joint tenant with right of survivorship" occurs if several are named on title and this "joint" language is written, then each owner has a percent share they can sell or gift during life but can't gift by Will since on death it goes to other owners;

d) "tenants by the entirety" occurs if 2 spouses in a marriage are named on title and this is specified or nothing else is said (the law "presumes" tenancy by the entirety for spouses), then a spouse has a half share they can't easily sell or gift during life or gift by Will and instead it goes to their spouse on death (this "entirety" ownership or sometimes "joint" ownership is often how spouses own their house);

e) a "life estate" occurs if title papers say so, then usually 1 person uses a property for their life but can't sell or gift in life or gift by Will since on death the property goes to others named on the title;

f) "trust property" occurs when paperwork creates a trust and people item by item transferred property into it, then only a "trustee" in charge can sell or gift trust property in ways the trust allows, and Wills can't usually affect trust property even if a Will maker use to own the property in the trust.

Property not real estate (like accounts) can be owned in these complex ways or by many people too.

IF THERE IS NO WILL THEN STATE "INTESTATE" LAW CONTROLS PROPERTY

"Intestate" means to die with no Will. If there is no Will then state intestate law says what happens to a "estate property" (property that did not transfer automatically on death), and the law says:

1) if a decedent has no descendants (like children or grandchildren) or surviving parents but has a spouse, a spouse gets 100%,

2) if a decedent has no surviving descendants but a surviving parent and a spouse, a spouse gets first $221,000 and 3/4th of rest,

3) if decedent had any surviving children shared with a surviving spouse, a spouse gets the first $221,000 plus 1/2 the rest, and

4) if decedent had surviving children but none were shared with a surviving spouse, the spouse gets first $148,00 plus 1/2 the rest.

The part of estate property not going to a spouse goes, in order, to a) descendants (children or grandchildren), b) surviving parents, c) other close relatives, and d) only if all that fails to the state.

FAMILY GET "HOMESTEAD", "EXEMPT PROPERTY", "MAINTENANCE" RIGHTS

Before most creditors owed by a decedent are paid and before a Will is carried out a decedent's family have rights to claim some of a decedent's property if they choose to ask for their rights.

"Homestead" allowance is a right to $22,000 cash which is raised by using a decedent's money or property, and this goes to a spouse or if no spouse then minor (under 18) and dependent children.

"Exempt Property" is a right to claim $15,000 of decedent's household items (like clothes, furniture, jewelry, tools, or vehicles), and some money and accounts if absolutely needed to reach $15,000 in value, and this goes to a spouse or if no spouse children (even if they are adults or not dependent).

"Family Allowance" is a right to support during any probate process, and often $27,000 cash is paid lump sum or in rare cases more, and which is raised by using a decedent's money or property, and this goes to a spouse or if no spouse minor and dependent children.

If a person has no surviving spouse or children these laws have no effect. Family rights together total $64,000, and change yearly a bit for inflation. If a family asks for family rights this uses up property and money so may interfere with Will gifts but this can only affect specific gifts in a Will (gifts where property is described) if there is no other property to use. Helpfully, if family in a Will get most things they often don't bother claiming family rights. <u>Basically, people should consider if family may claim some things using rights, so in a Will may need to be given less.</u> By special rule most debts of a funeral, burial, probate, and last illness have priority to be paid off before even family rights.

FAMILY RIGHTS IN RARE CASES CAN BE MODIFIED BY A CONTRACT OR WILL

In rare cases a lawyer's prenuptial or postnuptial contract spouses sign can give up a spouse's family rights. Or to avoid family getting Will gifts and also family rights (homestead, exempt property, and family allowance rights covered above in this book) some people add to Wills words like:

"Homestead, maintenance, and exempt property rights (MCL 700.2402, 700.2403, 700.2404) are included in and not in addition to the share of my estate and property passing by Will, and a personal representative shall reduce property or residue to a spouse or children for value of these they received."

Some add such words only in a Will's residue clause to reduce the share of the residue people get. If rights are limited usually they can still be used to help against creditors if an estate is small. This book's Wills do not limit these family rights since most people want them.

SPOUSE RATHER THAN FOLLOW WILL CAN CHOOSE "ELECTIVE SHARE"

State law says a spouse unhappy with what a Will gives them can instead elect an "Elective Share" of part of estate property of a decedent. This law is based on fairness and to avoid a spouse having to divorce to be certain of money for old age rather than stay married. The Elective Share a spouse can claim is: 1/2 the normal "intestate" share (what the law gives if no Will) reduced by 1/2 what a spouse got from a spouse outside probate (like from joint ownership, beneficiary forms, or gifts in last 2 years). Intestate shares are complex but (as said in this book) is at least the first $148,000 and 1/2 the rest; so an Elective Share is at least from estate property the first $74,000 plus 1/4 the rest. But homestead, exempt property, and maintenance rights which family rights usually total $64,000 can also be claimed and added if an Elective Share is used. Elective Share rights don't affect most "non-probate transfers" that give property on death to others, so these may affect things and a spouse worried about this maybe should see a lawyer. Since paying an Elective Share uses some of a decedent's property and money this may interfere with Will gifts, but to the degree possible others not a spouse still follow a Will. Basically, usually people doing a Will give a very large amount or share to any spouse to avoid them wanting to claim an Elective Share. In rare cases a lawyer's prenuptial or postnuptial contract spouses sign can give up Elective Share rights. In rare cases wives may have "dower" rights to use 1/3 of a decedent's real estate, but this is rare and usually any papers signed avoids this.

DEBTS ARE PAID BEFORE GIFTS IN WILL BUT NOT MORTGAGES OR LIENS

After any family rights claimed are paid creditors a decedent owed usually are paid next before Will gifts are carried out, like a decedent's bills, loans, credit cards, and family debts. Paying creditors uses some property and money so could interfere with Will gifts which people should plan for. To pay debts

1) first used is property passing by Will residue clause (which is property no other Will part used),

2) next used to pay debts is decedent's property in "general gifts" (like plain gifts of money), and

3) last used to pay debts is property in Will specific gifts (where property is specifically described).

Non-probate transfers may be stopped or undone only if all other property has been used to pay debts. State law does not pay off secured debts like mortgages or car liens, so people who get such property by Will or otherwise must keep paying a secured debt to keep the property. But Wills can be changed to say secured debts should be paid, like "Before gifts in this Will occur any debt on my 89 Buick and my property at 9 Rex Rd., Ivy, MI, is to be paid off". A simpler option is to give money to help pay a mortgage or lien. Family need not themselves pay debts they didn't co-sign or guarantee. A house owned by spouses as "tenants by the entirety" or jointly is usually safe from creditors owed by just a decedent not both spouses. In life usually to mortgage or sell real estate all spouses are asked to sign.

DO NEW WILL IF DIVORCE, MARRY, HAVE NEW CHILD, OR MOVE

Divorcing, marrying, having a new child, or moving to a new state after writing a Will can have big legal effects. If any of these occur it is recommended people do a new Will and review other papers.

AFTER A DEATH OCCURS THERE ARE SEVERAL PROBATE OPTIONS

After a death to help transfer property or do other thing there are many probate options.

Normal "supervised administration" probate in Michigan is fairly affordable but takes about 1 year.

"Unsupervised administration" has less paperwork and hearing than normal probate, is fairly affordable, and usually takes over 6-10 months. Most of this book's Wills allow this option.

"Small Estate" proceedings can be done to quickly transfer things to a spouse or descendants if estate property after funeral costs has a value less than $22,000 in 2015-2016.

"Affidavit of Decedent's Successor" forms can be used if there was no real estate left in the estate and under $22,000 in value in the estate in 2015-2016, which affidavits are easily filled out and given by a surviving spouse or descendants to anyone holding money or property.

Michigan "Certification From the Heir to a Vehicle" forms can be used to transfer vehicles or watercraft worth less than $60,000 to a spouse or descendants.

"Summary Proceeding" probate under MCL 700.3987 skips most normal probate steps and is available if property goes to a spouse or descendants and the estate value is below the total of the homestead, maintenance, and exempt property rights (these rights usually total $64,000).

If needed a safe deposit box can be looked in for a Will and similar documents using a special law.

Non-probate transfers often can be completed by showing of a death certificate, like land held with a joint tenant, transfer-on-death accounts, or investments that have a named beneficiary.

"Ancillary Probate" is a costly proceeding in another state needed for property there (usually real property), but this cost may be avoided by holding property in another state jointly with a person.

USUALLY NO FEDERAL OR MICHIGAN TAX IS OWED DUE TO A DEATH

Usually no tax is owed due to a death. First, the "Federal Estate And Gift Tax" taxes some gifts made during life or that occur on death, but this tax only starts when a tax credit is used up that covers $5,430,000 in transfers (this 2015-2016 amount will increase for inflation). Second, Michigan has no estate, inheritance, gift, or similar taxes. Third, another state's estate or inheritance tax can be owed for things located there or going to persons there, but few states have such taxes and they usually start at over $2,000,000. Most gifts to a U.S. spouse or to a charity like a church are free of all these taxes. A person's family or executor may have to file a last normal income tax or estate tax return.

CHAPTER 3
BASIC ISSUES IN WILLS AND GIFTING

"WILL" IS COMMON DOCUMENT TO CONTROL ISSUES AFTER DEATH

A "Will" is a common document that can be done by a person of sound mind at least age 18 to control many issues that may arise after their death. In Michigan to be valid a Will usually must be signed before 2 witnesses who then also sign. Issues in a Will can include who gets money and property, who will manage things as executor, if faster legal procedures can be used, and who if needed will be guardians of minor children and conservator of any minor's property. Not doing a Will can cause confusion, added costs, hearings, delays, and family fights. A Will is often called a "Last Will And Testament" and the person doing a Will is called a "Testator".

WILL CAN BE REVOKED BY NEW WILL, TEARING UP, OR MARKING

To cancel or "revoke" a Will a person can do a new Will which says it revokes previous Wills, or can personally do any act showing intent to revoke like tearing up, burning, or writing "canceled" on all pages. Revoking a Will does not usually bring back into force earlier Wills.

IN WILL CAN NAME "EXECUTOR" TO HANDLE MATTERS AFTER DEATH

Most Wills name an "executor" to after a death do some needed things like manage probate, find and transfer property and money, file any tax returns, pay bills, and settle creditor claims. An executor often is a spouse, adult child, or friend (or a lawyer or bank if they agree). An executor can be getting Will gifts, and can be named as guardian or conservator in a Will. If an executor needs a lawyer's help this is paid from a decedent's estate money and property. If needed and no Will names an executor a judge in a costly long costly hearing picks from a spouse and family who may argue. Naming 2 persons to be executor at the same time is allowed but less common due to possible legal problems and delays. An executor is paid back from estate property for fees and costs they pay. An executor can request compensation for hours of work they do, but asking for pay is often skipped as this uses up estate assets and is taxable income (unlike Will gifts). <u>Michigan officially now calls an executor a "Personal Representative"</u>, but the word "executor" is often used.

EXECUTOR HAS POWER TO EASILY COLLECT AND TRANSFER PROPERTY

An executor by law has power to easily collect and transfer most property and money of a decedent. Banks, investment companies, and others will usually follow instructions of an executor. Most Wills also have a part where executors are given more powers to help them do things.

WILL CAN SKIP EXECUTOR "BOND" AND ALLOW INFORMAL PROBATE

Most Wills say no "bond" or "surety" is required. This is insurance against executor misconduct paid for using estate funds, but most people do not want this cost since the executor is someone trusted. Also, most Wills say less formal probate called in Michigan "unsupervised administration" can be used, and all this book's Wills allow this.

WILL CAN NAME "GUARDIAN OF THE PERSON" TO CARE FOR CHILDREN

If a parent dies with a child under 18 the other natural or adopted parent (but not a step-parent) takes over automatically unless found "unfit" by a court which is rare. But in case it is needed a parent in a Will can name a "guardian of the person" to care for a child under 18, which choice a Michigan court must follow unless a person clearly would do bad. If no parent is available the person named guardian by Will files an "acceptance" at court, but a child 14 or older has a right ask for a court review. The preference of the last parent to die is given more weight. If needed and no Will names a guardian a judge in a costly long hearing picks from family who may argue about this. Naming 2 persons to be guardian at the same time is less common due to possible arguments and legal problems even if they are a married couple. Basically, in a Will since naming the other parent as guardian of the person is pointless (they take over unless unfit) most people name for this a healthy relative or friend. People without a child under 18 can skip or fill a guardian clause anyway, or use a Will without this like Form 3.

WILL CAN NAME "CONSERVATOR" TO MANAGE PROPERTY OF MINORS

In a Will a "conservator" can be named to manage property of those under 18 and decide how to use property to help pay for health care, schools, and living costs to 18 when anything left is handed over. By law persons under 18 can't control major property and banks and others may refuse to deal with them. Judges often follow a Will but can name a different person as conservator if it seems best. If needed and no Will names a conservator a judge in a costly hearing picks from a parent and family who may argue. Naming 2 persons to both be conservator is less common due to arguments and legal problems even if they are married. Often the "guardian of the person" is also named conservator unless they are bad with money (this avoids arguments and they know what should be paid for). Basically, usually when naming a conservator in a Will either 1) a minor will likely get things when a parent is still alive so a parent is named, or 2) a minor will likely get things only if all parents are dead so a friend or relative is named. A conservator does face work and costs each year of a court review looking for misuse. Due to added work and costs many people avoid giving to persons under 18, maybe gifting via family like "I give $80 to Ann Fox in the hope she will help her son Leo Fox". But a

11

helpful new law says a "custodian" process with less costs and work can manage a minor's property, and most of this book's Wills says a conservator can act like a custodian. Those without children under 18 and not giving things any minors can skip or fill in a conservator clause, or use a Will without this.

WILL CAN HAVE "ALTERNATE" EXECUTOR, GUARDIAN, AND CONSERVATOR

If a person named in a Will as executor, guardian, or conservator dies or is unavailable people can just write a new Will or a judge will pick someone if needed. But to plan ahead for the rare case someone dies or is unavailable people can modify a Will to name an "alternate" person, which is done by adding after a name: "or if they are reasonably unable to serve I nominate ___ to serve".

WILL HAS A FEW KINDS OF GIFTS TO SAY WHAT HAPPENS TO PROPERTY

Importantly, a Will is the normal way a person says what happens on death to their property and money. In a Will to make a gift often simple words are used, like "I give ___ to ___". After a death when Will gifts are carried out 1) Will "specific gifts" that name particular property are done first, 2) Will "general gifts" like money amounts are done next, and then 3) the Will "residue" gift is done last (which is basically anything remaining). Gifts of the same type usually occur in the order written in a Will. People should consider if gifts carried out earlier in a Will may leave less for later Will gifts.

IN A WILL CAN DO SPECIFIC GIFTS TO GIFT PARTICULAR PROPERTY

Most Wills in their main area have many "Specific Gift" sentences to let people gift particular property to persons named here. Specific gifts can be any kind of property like any clothing, furniture, tools, cars, investments, accounts, and real estate. Examples are: "I give Tin Goblets to Mary Dodd", "I give UBank account ending in 8473 to Ivy Dee", and "I give all clothing to Ann Coe". Specific gifts are given some preference and are carried out before most other Will gifts, and if possible the law tries to pay a decedent's debts and family rights not using things in specific gifts.

IN A WILL CAN DO GENERAL GIFTS OF MONEY AMOUNTS

Many people in a Will give general gifts of money amounts since this has less legal risk and problems. A "general gift" is a gift not involving specific property. "I give $90 to Ben Lee and Jan Kim" means the same as "I give a total of $90 to Ben Lee and Jan Kim" but using "total" is clearer. Later a court or executor will have power to use money in accounts or sell property to carry out money gifts. Even if a Will gifts money to a person a person can agree with an executor to take some property instead. Money gifts are often written with a Will's specific gifts but legally they are different.

12

"RESIDUE CLAUSE" IN WILL HELPFULLY GIVES ANYTHING LEFT OVER

Most Wills have a "residue clause" toward their end that helpfully gives any property of a person not given by other Will parts or by other means to persons named. This "catch-all" ensures everything goes to someone. Importantly, many people use a residue clause to give most their things since this has less legal risks and avoids having to describe property correctly. Often a Will's residue clause has:

1) a 1st space to name 1 or more persons to get things if they survive and are living at the Will maker's death (many name a spouse or closest family here), and

2) a 2nd space to name persons to get things if all people named in the 1st space don't survive (many name next closest family or friends here).

People should consider if debts to be paid, earlier gifts in a Will, and any non-probate transfers may leave little for the residue clause to give.

WILL GIFTS NOT OF MONEY ARE RISKIER AND CAN FAIL OR CHANGE

Will gifts not of money but of property items can change and even fail for many reasons, like a) property changing in value so some persons get far less value, b) property is sold by a person before death so is not owned to give, c) property is claimed by family using legal rights like "exempt property" rights, or d) property has to be sold to pay a decedent's debts. For many reasons in a Will rather than give particular property it may be better to give money amounts or, also, give using a Will "residue" clause (which gives all remaining property to persons named).

"CONDITIONS" CAN BE PUT ON A GIFT THAT MUST BE MET

"Conditions" can be put on a gift so if something does not occur the gift does not occur, like "I give all jewelry to Sue Lott if she loses 50 pounds" or "I give $90 to Amy Pond if she starts college". But gift conditions if strange or if timing is not kept short can lead to delay, lawsuits, and hurt feelings. Gift conditions against public policy like if based on race or too restrictive might be ignored.

THAT BENEFICIARY MUST "SURVIVE" TO GET GIFT IS USUAL CONDITION

Most Will gifts say "if they survive me" which means for a gift to occur the named beneficiary must be alive at the Will maker's death. A gift of no effect due to someone not surviving leaves the gifted property to follow later Will parts like a residue clause. To avoid legal problems most Wills define "survive" as outliving the Will maker by 60 days. If survival is not a gift condition then who gets a gift if a beneficiary has died depends on complex state law but sometimes it is the beneficiary's children.

ALTHOUGH RARELY NEEDED CAN NAME WILL "ALTERNATE BENEFICIARY"

For beneficiaries named to get Will gifts either 1) they survive to get the gift, 2) they don't survive but this is seen and a Will is rewritten, or 3) they don't survive and survival was a gift condition so property goes to who a person chose in a Will's residue clause (often a loved spouse or child). But if wanted a person can name an "alternate beneficiary" to get a gift if the named beneficiary does not survive as required. This is done in a gift by removing "if they survive me" and adding, "but if they fail to survive me then to_____", like "I give $9 to Ed Dee but if they fail to survive me then to Jo Wu".

FAMILY CAN BE ALTERNATE BENEFICIARY USING "LINEAL DESCENDANTS"

Although rarely needed (as explained above) one can have a person's descendants (usually children or grandchildren) be alternate beneficiaries in case the person doesn't survive to get a gift. This can be done by removing "if they survive me" gift language and adding there "or their lineal descendants per stirpes". The phrase "per stirpes" in the Latin language means "by the root" and means property is split among family branches and younger generations take for a dead parent. A spouse is not a "descendant" so "lineal descendants" language does not benefit them. An example is:

A man named Abe has 2 children Viv and Mort each of whom have 2 children. If Abe and Mort die and Abe's Will says "to Viv and Mort or lineal descendants per stirpes" the result is Viv gets 50% and Mort's 2 children each get 25%.

SEVERAL PERSONS CAN GET SAME PROPERTY OR MONEY TO SHARE

The same property or money can be gifted to several people to share, like "I give AmBank account ending in 8483 to Ed Coe and Jill Hill". Importantly, most Wills say for gifts to several persons if any have not survived other beneficiaries of the same gift take the non-survivor's share. Like, "I give $90 to Jan, Ada, and Kay Smith if they survive me" usually means if Ada has died the other 2 persons get $45. Most Wills say a gift will be sold and money passed on unless beneficiaries agree a gift's use.

BENEFICIARIES CAN GET PERCENTAGE RATHER THAN EQUAL SHARE

When several people get the same Will gift this usually means they get an equal share, but if wanted a percentage can be written to give such a share. Often a Will's "residue clause" is gifted by percentages to get the exact split wanted. Examples of Will gifts using percentages are:

"I give all cars 70% to Ed Coe and 30% to Max Dodd",

"I give 37 Dog St., Knox, MI, 90% to Tom Dee and 10% to Ned Bund", and

"I give the residue 70% to Janet Ann Nox my wife, 20% to John Eric Nox, and 10% to Erin Joy Hill".

14

NEED SUFFICIENT DESCRIPTION OF PERSONS NAMED IN WILL

People named in a Will must be described with enough detail. The person doing a Will usually writes their full legal name in all places including when signing. Some people add they are known by another name but this is not required (like, "I am also known as Bear Smith" or "a/k/a Bear Smith"). Descriptions of beneficiaries getting Will gifts just needs enough detail so people who knew a decedent can tell who probably is meant, so often a partial name or nickname is enough. Wills can skip names if who is in a group is clear, like "I give $95 to each of my sister Kim's kids". It can help to say how a person is known, but in most cases using a full name in a gift is fine and is standard. For a pet many give a pet and money for care to a trusted friend (like, "I give my cat Kiki and $90 to Jo Dee") or a lawyer's "Pet Trust" can be done for a pet. Examples of describing beneficiaries in Will gifts are:

"I give $95 to Tom Smith my mechanic",

"I give my boat to Big Bjorg",

"I give $800 to Bloomington Happy Meals the food charity in town", and

"I give $8 to Greg Paul Coe".

NEED SUFFICIENT DESCRIPTION OF PROPERTY GIFTED IN WILL

Property in a Will gift must be described so those who knew a decedent can tell the likely meaning. This is easy as most people only own 1 of something. It is OK to describe property by category, by standard location, or to have a long list of property in a single gift. For real property using an absolutely correct "legal description" is best (like "Lot 2, Block 4 of Polk's Addition to Boyd") but using a street address is allowed. Examples of describing property in Will gifts are:

"I give tools usually kept in my garage to Ron Hull",

"I give my biggest gold ring to Vera Kline",

"I give Ubank account ending #9283 to Mary Bing", and

"I give 92 Lake St., Ford, Michigan, including land, buildings, and fixtures, to Ann Joy Hull".

WILLS IGNORE PLURAL AND GENDER OF WORDS

Wills often say plural or gender meanings of words are ignored, which lets people write in anything wanted. Often Wills use "they" when it may refer to 1 person, like "I give ___ to ___ if they survive me".

WILLS HAVE LONG "MISCELLANEOUS" SECTION TO HELP AVOID PROBLEMS

Most Wills have a long "Miscellaneous" section with many sentences of legal language that help avoid some possible legal problems and which explain parts of the Will.

LISTS OUTSIDE A WILL CAN GIVE "TANGIBLE PERSONAL PROPERTY"

Michigan lets people write gifts of tangible personal property to happen on their death in simple lists separate from a Will. "Tangible personal property" includes things like clothing, furniture, jewelry, appliances, tools, and vehicles. People can write many lists but is better if they do just 1 big list. This book's Chapter 8 explains lists more and has Form 4 the "Tangible Personal Property List" form.

WILL CAN BE SUPPPORTED BY SELF-PROVING AFFIDAVIT

Any Will can be supported a "Self-Proving Affidavit" form, including the Wills in Form 1, Form 2, and Form 3 in this book. The Self-Proving Affidavit form is Form 4 in this book in Chapter 7.

KEEP SIGNED WILL IN SAFE PLACE IT CAN BE FOUND

When signed a Will should be stapled together and kept in a safe place where it can be found within days of a death like a desk, filing cabinet, a safe or safe deposit box (if possible share access), or with a trusted person like spouse or friend (or tell them where to look). For safekeeping a Will can be filed at a local court and can be withdrawn if wanted (usually tell family a Will has been filed).

"HOLOGRAPHIC" WILL WITHOUT WITNESSES IS NOT RECOMMENDED

Normally a Will must be signed before 2 witnesses who then sign too, but Michigan law allows Wills done wholly or mostly in a person's handwriting to be signed with no witnesses, which is called a "Holographic Will". Such Wills to be valid must be dated, signed, the intent and meaning must be clear, and all material portions must be in a person's own handwriting. But it can be hard to handwrite several Will pages without either making mistakes, using confusing language, or leaving out helpful language most Wills have. A Holographic Will without witnesses is not recommended and rarely done.

IN GENERAL GIFT AS WANTED, KEEP IT SIMPLE, AND CONSIDER A SPOUSE

Under Michigan law a person is mostly free to gift their property and money as wanted including giving nothing to a child. In a Will despite having many options it is usually best to keep gifting simple. For example, in a Will it may be best to first make a few small gifts (gifts of money not specific property have less legal problems), and second use a Will's residue clause to give all else to a person or a few people. But if a person has a spouse the spouse may need resources to live on, so most people give any spouse most things in a Will and in other ways. Some people also give a spouse informal instructions about what to do with some property which they trust will be followed. If people later survive a spouse they can do a new Will that switches to giving more to other persons.

CHAPTER 4
FORM 1: MICHIGAN STATUTORY WILL

PEOPLE CAN DO A WILL TO CONTROL THINGS AFTER THEIR DEATH

As explained in this book a "Will" is a common document done by a person to control issues that may arise after their death. A Will is often called a "Last Will And Testament" and a person doing a Will is called a "Testator". Anyone at least 18 and of sound mind can do a Will.

"STATUTORY WILL" IS SHORT EFFECTIVE WILL BUT DO NOT MODIFY IT

Form 1 is the "Michigan Statutory Will" which is a short effective Will form written by the legislature to help most people and found in law at MCL 700.2519. The Michigan Statutory Will is known to judges and guaranteed to have no legal problems, and it is recommended people use this if they can. "Instructions" to explain the Will come before its main parts, and in this book a helpful "Questions & Answers" article from the Michigan.gov website appears after it. Unlike other Wills by law a person cannot remove or modify language in the Michigan Statutory Will and doing this may make it invalid.

WILL GIVES 2 CASH GIFTS, LISTS, AND REST TO SPOUSE OR CHILDREN

The Michigan Statutory Will has only a few gifting options but they should be enough for most.

First, the Will has a place to give 2 gifts of money to a person or charity, with no dollar limit.

Second, the Will says any separate "lists" giving household items, jewelry, or automobiles should be followed if a person ever writes such lists, with no limit on the total that can be given. People who want can use this book's Form 5 "Tangible Personal Property List" form to write such lists.

Third, the Will says all else is given to any spouse, and if no spouse then to any children (or to grandchildren if a Will maker's child has died but left grandchildren to take their share).

Fourth, for the very rare case things have not been distributed (which happens only if there is no spouse, child, or grandchild of a person) the Will lets a person choose if things then go to:
a) their family alone, or b) 1/2 to their last spouse's family too.

Most people can reach most of their goals using this Will. For example, a) people can use the 2 money gifts to give money to more elderly people, b) use lists to give items of property to people fit enough to use the items or sell the items, and c) whatever is left under the Will's wording goes to a spouse or if no spouse to children. But with this Will if there is a spouse any children get nothing unless people remember to write gifts for them. And with this Will if a person named to get a gift dies who gets the gift depends on complex legal factors (so most people redo a Will if someone in it dies).

WILL NAMES EXECUTOR, GUARDIAN, AND CONSERVATOR AND COVERS BOND

The Michigan Statutory Will has a place to name an executor (called a "personal representative"), guardian of children, and a conservator of any minor's property. People can skip some of these if they seems unneeded, but there is no harm in doing them. There is a place to say whether a "bond" has to be gotten to insure against misconduct of the executor, guardian, and conservator, and most people skip bonds since those chosen are trusted and a bond is paid for with the deceased person's property.

COMPLETE BY PERSON SIGNING BEFORE 2 OR 3 WITNESSES WHO SIGN TOO

To be valid the Michigan Statutory Will form must be signed by the person doing the Will with at least 2 witnesses present who then sign too. The form suggests a 3rd witness be used too and has a space for this but this is not standard. It is not required but often the person making the Will holds the Will up and says things to witnesses like, "This is the Will I want and want you to witness me signing". Witnesses usually read only the "Statement Of Witnesses" next to where they sign. Witnesses must be at least 18 and if possible should be young so likely to be available later if needed. Witnesses can can be family of the Will maker, named executor or guardian or conservator in the form, and getting gifts in the Will, but it is a bit better if people without these connections are used as witnesses.

FORM 1:
MICHIGAN STATUTORY WILL

MICHIGAN STATUTORY WILL NOTICE

1. An individual age 18 or older and of sound mind may sign a will.

2. There are several kinds of wills. If you choose to complete this form, you will have a Michigan statutory will. If this will does not meet your wishes in any way, you should talk with a lawyer before choosing a Michigan statutory will.

3. Warning! It is strongly recommended that you do not add or cross out any words on this form except for filling in the blanks because all or part of this will may not be valid if you do so.

4. This will has no effect on jointly held assets, on retirement plan benefits, or on life insurance on your life if you have named a beneficiary who survives you.

5. This will is not designed to reduce estate taxes.

6. This will treats adopted children and children born outside of wedlock who would inherit if their parent died without a will the same way as children born or conceived during marriage.

7. You should keep this will in your safe deposit box or other safe place. By paying a small fee, you may file this will in your county's probate court for safekeeping. You should tell your family where the will is kept.

8. You may make and sign a new will at any time. If you marry or divorce after you sign this will, you should make and sign a new will.

INSTRUCTIONS:

1. To have a Michigan statutory will, you must complete the blanks on the will form. You may do this yourself, or direct someone to do it for you. You must either sign the will or direct someone else to sign it in your name and in your presence.

2. Read the entire Michigan statutory will carefully before you begin filling in the blanks. If there is anything you do not understand, you should ask a lawyer to explain it to you.

MICHIGAN STATUTORY WILL OF _____

(Print or type your full name)

ARTICLE 1. DECLARATIONS

This is my will and I revoke any prior wills and codicils.

I live in _____ County, Michigan.

My spouse is _____.

(Insert spouse's name or write "none")

My children now living are:

_____   _____

_____   _____

_____   _____

(Insert names or write "none")

ARTICLE 2. DISPOSITION OF MY ASSETS

2.1 CASH GIFTS TO PERSONS OR CHARITIES.

(Optional)

I can leave no more than two (2) cash gifts. I make the following cash gifts to the persons or charities in the amount stated here. Any transfer tax due upon my death shall be paid from the balance of my estate and not from these gifts.

Full name and address of person or charity to receive cash gift (name only 1 person or charity here):

_____

(Insert name of person or charity)

_____

(Insert address)

AMOUNT OF GIFT (In figures): $_____

AMOUNT OF GIFT (In words): _____ Dollars

_____

(Your signature)

Full name and address of person or charity to receive cash gift (name only 1 person or charity here):

_____

(Insert name of person or charity)

_____

(Insert address)

AMOUNT OF GIFT (In figures): $_____

AMOUNT OF GIFT (In words): _____ Dollars

_____

(Your signature)

2.2 PERSONAL AND HOUSEHOLD ITEMS.

I may leave a separate list or statement, either in my handwriting or signed by me at the end, regarding gifts of specific books, jewelry, clothing, automobiles, furniture, and other personal and household items.

I give my spouse all my books, jewelry, clothing, automobiles, furniture, and other personal and household items not included on such a separate list or statement. If I am not married at the time I sign this will or if my spouse dies before me, my personal representative shall distribute those items, as equally as possible, among my children who survive me. If no children survive me, these items shall be distributed as set forth in paragraph 2.3.

2.3 ALL OTHER ASSETS.

I give everything else I own to my spouse. If I am not married at the time I sign this will or if my spouse dies before me, I give these assets to my children and the descendants of any deceased child. If no spouse, children, or descendants of children survive me, I choose 1 of the following distribution clauses by signing my name on the line after that clause. If I sign on both lines, if I fail to sign on either line, or if I am not now married, these assets will go under distribution clause (b).

Distribution clause, if no spouse, children, or descendants of children survive me.

(Select only 1)

(a) One-half to be distributed to my heirs as if I did not have a will, and one-half to be distributed to my spouse's heirs as if my spouse had died just after me without a will.

_____
(Your signature)

(b) All to be distributed to my heirs as if I did not have a will.

_____
(Your signature)

ARTICLE 3. NOMINATIONS OF PERSONAL REPRESENTATIVE, GUARDIAN, AND CONSERVATOR

Personal representatives, guardians, and conservators have a great deal of responsibility. The role of a personal representative is to collect your assets, pay debts and taxes from those assets, and distribute the remaining assets as directed in the will. A guardian is a person who will look after the physical well-being of a child. A conservator is a person who will manage a child's assets and make payments from those assets for the child's benefit. Select them carefully. Also, before you select them, ask them whether they are willing and able to serve.

3.1 PERSONAL REPRESENTATIVE.

(Name at least 1)

I nominate _____ of
　　　　　　　(Insert name of person or eligible financial institution)
_____ to serve as personal representative.
　　　　(Insert address)

If my first choice does not serve, I nominate _____
　　　　　　　　　　　　　　　　　　　　　(Insert name of person or eligible financial institution)
of _____ to serve as personal representative.
　　　　(Insert address)

3.2 GUARDIAN AND CONSERVATOR.

Your spouse may die before you. Therefore, if you have a child under age 18, name an individual as guardian of the child, and an individual or eligible financial institution as conservator of the child's assets. The guardian and the conservator may, but need not be, the same person.

If a guardian or conservator is needed for a child of mine, I nominate

_____ of _____
(Insert name of individual)   (Insert address)

as guardian and _____
(Insert name of individual or eligible financial institution)

of _____ to serve as conservator.
(Insert address)

If my first choice cannot serve, I nominate _____
(Insert name of individual)

of _____
(Insert address)

as guardian and _____
(Insert name of individual or eligible financial institution)

of _____ to serve as conservator.
(Insert address)

3.3 BOND.

A bond is a form of insurance in case your personal representative or a conservator performs improperly and jeopardizes your assets. A bond is not required. You may choose whether you wish to require your personal representative and any conservator to serve with or without bond. Bond premiums would be paid out of your assets. (Select only 1)

(a) My personal representative and any conservator I have named shall serve with bond.

_____
(Your signature)

(b) My personal representative and any conservator I have named shall serve without bond.

_____
(Your signature)

3.4 DEFINITIONS AND ADDITIONAL CLAUSES.

Definitions and additional clauses found at the end of this form are part of this will.

I sign my name to this Michigan statutory will on _____, 20___.

_____
(Your signature)

NOTICE REGARDING WITNESSES

You must use 2 adults who will not receive assets under this will as witnesses. It is preferable to have 3 adult witnesses. All the witnesses must observe you sign the will, have you tell them you signed the will, or have you tell them the will was signed at your direction in your presence.

STATEMENT OF WITNESSES

We sign below as witnesses, declaring that the individual who is making this will appears to be of sound mind and appears to be making this will freely, without duress, fraud, or undue influence, and that the individual making this will acknowledges that he or she has read the will, or has had it read to him or her, and understands the contents of this will.

_____

(Print name)

_____

(Signature of witness)

_____

(Address)

_____   _____   _____

(City)   (State)   (Zip)

_____

(Print name)

_____

(Signature of witness)

_____

(Address)

_____   _____   _____

(City)   (State)   (Zip)

_____

(Print name)

_____

(Signature of witness)

_____

(Address)

_____   _____   _____

(City)   (State)   (Zip)

DEFINITIONS

The following definitions & rules of construction apply to this Michigan statutory will:

(a) "Assets" means all types of property you can own, such as real estate, stocks and bonds, bank accounts, business interests, furniture, and automobiles.

(b) "Descendants" means your children, grandchildren, and their descendants.

(c) "Descendants" or "children" includes individuals born or conceived during marriage, individuals legally adopted, and individuals born out of wedlock who would inherit if their parent died without a will.

(d) "Jointly held assets" means those assets to which ownership is transferred automatically upon the death of 1 of the owners to the remaining owner or owners.

(e) "Spouse" means your husband or wife at the time you sign this will.

(f) Whenever a distribution under a Michigan statutory will is to be made to an individual's descendants, the assets are to be divided into as many equal shares as there are then living descendants of the nearest degree of living descendants and deceased descendants of that same degree who leave living descendants. Each living descendant of the nearest degree shall receive 1 share. The remaining shares, if any, are combined and then divided in the same manner among the surviving descendants of the deceased descendants as if the surviving descendants who were allocated a share and their surviving descendants had predeceased the descendant. In this manner, all descendants who are in the same generation will take an equal share.

(g) "Heirs" means those persons who would have received your assets if you had died without a will, domiciled in Michigan, under the laws that are then in effect.

(h) "Person" includes individuals and institutions.

(i) Plural and singular words include each other, where appropriate.

(j) If a Michigan statutory will states that a person shall perform an act, the person is required to perform that act. If a Michigan statutory will states that a person may do an act, the person's decision to do or not to do the act shall be made in good faith exercise of the person's powers.

ADDITIONAL CLAUSES
Powers of Personal Representative

1. A personal representative has all powers of administration given by Michigan law to personal representatives and, to the extent funds are not needed to meet debts and expenses currently payable and are not immediately distributable, the power to invest and reinvest the estate from time to time in accordance with the Michigan prudent investor rule. In dividing and distributing the estate, the personal representative may distribute partially or totally in kind, may determine the value of distributions in kind without reference to income tax bases, and may make non-pro rata distributions.

2. The personal representative may distribute estate assets otherwise distributable to a minor beneficiary to the minor's conservator or, in amounts not exceeding $5,000.00 per year, either to the minor, if married; to a parent or another adult with whom the minor resides and who has the care, custody, or control of the minor, or to the guardian. The personal representative is free of liability and is discharged from further accountability for distributing assets in compliance with the provisions of this paragraph.

POWERS OF GUARDIAN AND CONSERVATOR

A guardian named in this will has the same authority with respect to the child as a parent having legal custody would have. A conservator named in this will has all of the powers conferred by law.

<u>MICHIGAN.GOV ANSWERS ABOUT STATUTORY WILLS</u>

(The following helpful information is not part of Statutory Will form)

What happens if I die without a will? With certain exceptions, your possessions are divided according to state law among your closest relatives. You are said to die "intestate."

What can I accomplish by making out a will? You can choose who is to receive your property; select someone to serve as personal representative (formerly known as executor); and appoint a guardian for your children under age 18. A person who dies having made a valid will is said to have died "testate."

If I have a will, do I avoid probate? No. Whether or not you die with a will, your property will usually go through probate, which is a process through which the probate court oversees distribution of your assets. If there is a will, the initial purpose of probate is to prove that the will is valid.

Does all property go through probate? No. For example, money held in a joint bank account automatically belongs to the other owner. If your spouse's or child's name is on the deed to your house, the house automatically belongs to him or her. Life insurance benefits go directly to the beneficiary named in the policy. A will has no effect on these types of property, which are known collectively as the "non-probate" estate.

If property is specified in my will, can I give it away or sell it during my life? Yes. Your will has no effect until you die. If you have sold or given away property mentioned in the will, that provision of the will is ignored; this has no effect on the rest of your will.

Are there different types of wills? Yes. There are handwritten wills, typewritten wills, and statutory wills. Each type is equally valid if done precisely in accordance with the law. It is recommended you see a lawyer if you do not use the statutory will.

What can I accomplish through using a statutory will? (a) You can leave up to two cash gifts of any amount to people or charities. (b) You can write a list of personal and household items, and name who is to receive each item. (c) The rest of your property goes to your husband or wife. If he or she dies before you, this property would be divided equally among your children. (d) You can select a personal representative to administer your property. (e) You can appoint a guardian and conservator in case you and your spouse both die before your children reach age 18.

Are there any reasons for me NOT to use the statutory will? There may be. If you have substantial wealth and need tax planning for your estate, you should consult a lawyer who handles estate planning and probate. If you think you might have such problems, speak with a lawyer to see if more complex planning is indicated. Consultation with a lawyer is strongly recommended if you want to establish a trust fund for your children's education, if you have assets outside Michigan, or if you have a significant interest in a business partnership.

I have a wife and two young children. Might a statutory will be appropriate for my purposes? Perhaps. A statutory will might be appropriate if you do not have extensive assets and, therefore, do not need tax planning. In a statutory will, you can appoint a guardian for your children and a conservator for your children's assets.

I would like to leave my favorite niece an antique brooch. Can I do this with a statutory will? Yes. A statutory will allows you to leave gifts of personal items by making a list of the items and the person you want to receive each item.

I am a widow with no children. Could a statutory will be appropriate for me? If you do not have substantial assets and you do not object to the limited options for disposing of your property, you may want to use the simple statutory form.

I own a house, a condominium, and much stock. Should I use a statutory will? Perhaps not. A statutory will is not designed to reduce federal or state taxes on your estate. If you have very substantial assets, check with a lawyer to see if tax planning is recommended.

I am married for the second time and my husband and I each have children from our first marriages. Would a statutory will be appropriate for my purposes? Probably not. The statutory will provides that your estate goes to your husband if he survives you. The statutory will does not give you an adequate way to provide for the children from your first marriage. Speaking with a lawyer is a good idea for someone in a second marriage.

I have rather complicated business interests, which I wish to pass on through my will. Would a statutory will be appropriate for my purposes? No. A statutory will does not provide for any specific business planning.

What should I do if a statutory will doesn't meet my needs? Contact a lawyer with knowledge of estate planning. He or she can draft a will to meet your specific needs.

How can I find a good lawyer? There is no sure-fire way. Here are some suggestions: (a) If you have dealt with a lawyer in the past and were satisfied, go back to that person. A lawyer who does not handle estate planning will be happy to recommend someone who does. (b) Ask friends, neighbors, or relatives for someone they have been pleased with. (c) Ask a person you respect, such as a religious leader, or call an organization such as a consumer group or your labor union. (d) Call the county or state bar referral service, which will provide you with the names of two or three lawyers. (e) Consult the yellow pages of newspaper classified section. Don't be intimidated. Don't be afraid to "shop around" for someone you are comfortable with and whose services you can afford.

How do I proceed to use the statutory will form? First, thoroughly read the entire form. Read the notice at the beginning and the definitions at the end. After you are sure you understand all of the will's provisions, carefully follow directions and fill in the blanks. In reading over the form, the following questions may arise.

May I use a statutory will form and yet leave no cash gifts? (Article 2.1) Yes. You may leave no cash gifts, one cash gift, or two cash gifts. If you do leave a cash gift, it is important that you give a complete address for the person or charity to receive the money.

How do I go about preparing a list of personal items? (Article 2.2) If you wish, you may make a list on a separate piece of paper of possessions such as jewelry, books, automobiles, furniture, and other personal and household items. On the list you name who is to receive each item - a family member, friend, or neighbor. The list can be as short or long as you choose. Make sure you describe each item sufficiently to avoid confusion. For each person who is to get an item, include his or her full name and address. The list must be in your handwriting or signed by you. It is a very good idea to include the date. You may make the list before you complete the statutory will form, at the same time, or afterward. You can change the list as often as you wish. It is a good idea to staple or firmly attach the newest list to your will.

What is the purpose of Article 2.3? This provision sets out the division of your property (other than cash gifts and the list of items) if your spouse, children, grandchildren and great-grandchildren all die before you.

Need I complete Article 3.2 if all of my children are over 18? No. You may skip Article 3.2 relating to guardians and conservators.

How do I decide whether to have my personal representative serve with or without bond? (Article 3.3) Most people these days request that the personal representative serve without bond. If you are careful to choose a person you trust to be personal representative, there seems little need to spend your money for a bond.

Who may be a witness to my will? Any adult who will not receive any possessions or money under your will may be a witness. This is important. A person who may receive money or property under your will should never be a witness to your will. You need not tell witnesses about the contents of your will.

After the will is completed, where should I keep it? One option is to file it in probate court at the cost of $5.00. Wherever you keep the will, it is a good idea to attach the list of personal items to the will. You may want to give a copy of the will to the person you have selected as personal representative.

Can I make changes to my statutory will? Yes. Since a will has absolutely no effect until you die, you can change the will during your life. But do not write on the will. You can either have a codicil (amendment) drafted, complete a new statutory will, or have an entire new will drafted by a lawyer. If you sign a new will, destroy copies of the old one. You can change the list of personal property items at any time. It is probably best to write a whole new list if you decide to make changes.

If I move from Michigan would my statutory will still be valid? Probably yes. It would be a good idea to check with a lawyer who practices law in the state of your new residence.

CHAPTER 5
FORM 2: LAST WILL AND TESTAMENT (WITH GUARDIANS)

THIS BOOK'S 3 WILL FORMS SHOULD HELP MOST WITHOUT ANY CHANGES

As explained in this book a "Will" is a common document done by a person to control issues after their death. This book's forms show with blank spaces and underlining where most words, signatures, and dates should be added. This book's writing does show some ways to add legal language or modify words in forms, but changing forms is rarely needed and can by risky to do.

FORM 2 IS A FLEXIBLE WILL WITH A GUARDIANS PARAGRAPH

The Will in Form 2 is flexible and lets people write in whatever gifts they want. Also the Will in Form 2 has a "Guardians" paragraph to name a "guardian of the person" to if needed care for a child under 18 and also name a "conservator" to if needed manage any minor's property until 18. People with no children under 18 and also not giving anything to a person under 18 when at to the guardians paragraph can skip it or fill it in anyway, or use the Will in Form 3 which has no Guardians paragraph.

WILL IN FORM 2 HAS BASIC LAYOUT WITH SEVERAL PARTS

The Will in Form 2 has a basic layout. Right at its start there is a place for the person making the Will to write their full legal name and last county of residence in Michigan.

The 1st paragraph, "Gifts", has many spaces to make either specific gifts of particular property or to make gifts of money amounts.

The 2nd paragraph, "Tangible Personal Property List", says to follow any such lists people ever do.

The 3rd paragraph, "Residue", has a "residue" clause to give anything not given by other parts of the Will or in other ways to whoever is named here (many people use this to give most things).

The 4th paragraph, "Administration", has space to name a person as "executor" (also called "personal representative") to handle some matters after someone's death.

The 5th paragraph, "Guardians", lets a person name a "guardian of the person" to if needed care for a child under 18 and a "conservator" to if needed manage any minor's property until 18.

The 6th paragraph, "Miscellaneous", is made up of many sentences of legal language written to help avoid certain legal problems and to explain the Will.

Last in the form is a place for the person doing the Will to sign, and a place for 2 witnesses to sign.

RESIDUE CLAUSE HAS 2 PLACES TO NAME PERSONS TO GET THINGS

In a Will's "residue clause" anything not given by other parts of the Will or other means is gifted to the persons named in the clause. A residue clause is a "catch-all" making sure all property and money goes to someone. Many people use a residue clause to gift most their things since this is easy, avoids having to describe property, and has less legal risk. This Will's residue clause is written to have:

1) a 1st space to name 1 or more persons to get the residue (but any named here must survive to get things or their share goes to others named here), and

2) a 2nd space to name people to get things if all in the 1st space don't survive (any named here who don't survive have their share go to descendants and not others named here).

Most people name in the 1st space a spouse or closest family, and in the 2nd space most people name their next closest family or friends. Very helpful options exist to use with the residue clause:

a) People can in the residue clause leave the 1st space empty and only name people in the 2nd space to ensure if someone named dies their descendants get their share;

b) People can repeat names in the 2 clause spaces if there is only 1 person or group to target;

c) People can in either of the residue clause's spaces gift by percentages.

This residue clause may seem complex but usually whoever is named in the 1st used space gets things if they are living when the Will maker dies.

WILL IS DONE BY TESTATOR AND 2 WITNESSES COMPLETING PARAGRAPHS

Wills are completed by the person doing the Will (called the "Testator") signing a "Testator" paragraph in front of 2 witnesses, and then 2 witnesses signing a "Witnesses" paragraph and writing their addresses in front of each other and Testator. Full names should be used. Some people hold up their Will and say to witnesses things like, "This is the Will I want and want you to witness". In the paragraphs people sign a person can write in their own names and the date, or anyone can fill this in beforehand. Wills have some words about "perjury" and this book's Chapter 7 explains this. Most witnesses do not look at a Will except to read the paragraph they sign. Witnesses can be family, getting Will gifts, or the executor or guardian or conservator, but it is best if witnesses are not connected in these ways. Witnesses must be over 18, but if possible not too old. All who sign should see the other's hands as they sign using a permanent pen or marker. To fight forgery or help with proof some people modify Wills to have spots to initial each page or have more than 2 witnesses.

FORM 2:
LAST WILL AND TESTAMENT (WITH GUARDIANS)

LAST WILL AND TESTAMENT

I, _____ a resident of _____ County, Michigan, hereby make, publish, and declare this as my Last Will and Testament (called here my "Will"), and I hereby revoke any Wills and Codicils earlier made by me.

1. GIFTS. I give the following gifts which are specific gifts except any gifts of money amounts are general gifts:

I give _____ to _____ if they survive me;

I give _____ to _____ if they survive me;

I give _____ to _____ if they survive me;

I give _____ to _____ if they survive me;

I give _____ to _____ if they survive me;

I give _____ to _____ if they survive me;

I give _____ to _____ if they survive me;

I give _____ to _____ if they survive me;

I give _____ to _____ if they survive me;

and I give _____ to _____ if they survive me.

2. TANGIBLE PERSONAL PROPERTY LIST. If a list or written statement signed or handwritten by me gives tangible personal property as allowed by law including Michigan law at MCL 700.2513 then I make such gifts. All such writing are intended to be and are to be construed as part of one document to all be followed. If any property is given in multiple writings the page that appears most recently completed controls. But any such writings not found by 60 days after my death and the gifts in such writings shall abate and have no effect.

FORM 2:
LAST WILL AND TESTAMENT (WITH GUARDIANS)

LAST WILL AND TESTAMENT

I, _____ a resident of _____ County, Michigan, hereby make, publish, and declare this as my Last Will and Testament (called here my "Will"), and I hereby revoke any Wills and Codicils earlier made by me.

1. GIFTS. I give the following gifts which are specific gifts except any gifts of money amounts are general gifts:

I give _____ to _____ if they survive me;

I give _____ to _____ if they survive me;

I give _____ to _____ if they survive me;

I give _____ to _____ if they survive me;

I give _____ to _____ if they survive me;

I give _____ to _____ if they survive me;

I give _____ to _____ if they survive me;

I give _____ to _____ if they survive me;

I give _____ to _____ if they survive me;

and I give _____ to _____ if they survive me.

2. TANGIBLE PERSONAL PROPERTY LIST. If a list or written statement signed or handwritten by me gives tangible personal property as allowed by law including Michigan law at MCL 700.2513 then I make such gifts. All such writing are intended to be and are to be construed as part of one document to all be followed. If any property is given in multiple writings the page that appears most recently completed controls. But any such writings not found by 60 days after my death and the gifts in such writings shall abate and have no effect.

3. RESIDUE. I give all property not given or used by other Will provisions, and the rest, residue, and remainder of my estate, whether now owned or later acquired, wherever located, and of any kind and nature including personal, real, and mixed property, including all property which I die possessed or am in any way entitled (all of which is called the "residue" in this Will), as follows: to _____ if they survive me, but if they all do not survive me then I give the just described property to _____ or their lineal descendants per stirpes.

4. ADMINISTRATION. I name and appoint _____ as personal representative of my Will and my estate, also called "executor" in this Will.

5. GUARDIANS. If any of my children have not reached age 18 I name and appoint _____ to be guardian of such children including of their person. I also name and appoint _____ to be conservator of the estate of such children and their property or other persons under age 18 who receive or possess property.

6. MISCELLANEOUS. The following applies to this Will and generally.

I direct unsupervised administration of my estate and Will or less burdensome options.

Plural, singular, or gender meanings do not limit Will provisions, including use of "they".

Any personal representative, guardian of any type, and conservator serving under this Will or otherwise shall serve without bond, surety, or other security.

A gift shall be sold unless all beneficiaries getting a gift agree on how to use or sell a gift.

If a beneficiary does not survive then their share goes to any other beneficiaries of the gift in proportion to the share they are getting, including the residue and if a gift says survival is required and despite anti-lapse or similar laws, but not if an alternate beneficiary is provided.

No unfilled Will part or blank is a mistake or incomplete, including for the residue.

Priority of Will gifts of the same type is based on the order they appear in this Will.

"Give" and "gift" means the same as devise, bequest, grant, legacy or similar.

"Survive" or "surviving" means to not stop living before 60 days after my death, and if in a gift is an absolute condition that must be met and anti-lapse or similar laws have no effect.

In addition to powers given by MCL 700.3715, any personal representative, guardian, and conservator is given as much power, authority, and discretion that may be given by law, including power to do any acts any personal representative finds may be helpful.

Any personal representative shall have power to with no liability for change in value lease, assign, sell at public or private sale with or without public notice, mortgage, hold, invest, abandon, encumber, exchange, manage, operate, and transfer in any way any property including of the estate, settle claims for and against the estate or any person, and have power of sale over real property, all with no need for involvement or permission or act of a court or other party at any time, and all with no need for any filing or inventory or other thing.

Any personal representative has power to at any time pay debts of any amount of mine or my estate that they in their sole and absolute discretion find valid and timely and fair, like debts of a last illness or funeral or burial, with no inventory or filing or any court action.

Any personal representative has power to petition for, appoint a fiduciary for, or pay for ancillary estate action, transact with my estate or any trust without act of any person or court, give different kinds, portions or undivided interests in property to beneficiaries and assign value to all things, and do any distribution or division of my estate or property in cash or in kind.

For gifts or property going to a minor any personal representative without act of a court has power to choose to and make transfers to: the minor, conservator named by Will or court, or custodian under the Michigan Uniform Transfers to Minors Act or other law. Persons named conservator in this Will are hereby nominated custodian for such minors under the Michigan Uniform Transfers to Minors Act, or a personal representative may appoint a custodian.

Failure to make gifts to some family including children is intentional and not a mistake.

The residue includes lapsed or failed gifts, insurance paid to the estate, and property a testator had a power of appointment or testamentary disposition over.

<u>TESTATOR</u>

I, who am named _____, the Testator, sign my name to this document on _____, 20__, and I declare under penalty for perjury under the law of the state of Michigan that the following statements are true: this document is my Will; I sign it willingly; I sign it as my voluntary act for the purposes expressed in it; I am at least 18 years old, have sufficient mental capacity to make this Will, and am under no constraint or undue influence.

_____
Testator

<u>WITNESSES</u>

We, who are named _____ and _____, the Witnesses, sign our names to this document on _____, 20__, and we declare under penalty for perjury under the law of the state of Michigan that the following statements are true: the person signing this document as the Testator signs the document as his or her Will, signs it willingly, and executes it as his or her voluntary act for the purposes expressed in this Will; each of us in the Testator's presence signs this Will as witness to the Testator's signing; and to the best of our knowledge the Testator is at least 18 years old, has sufficient mental capacity to make this Will, and is under no constraint or undue influence.

_____   _____
Witness   Address

_____   _____
Witness   Address

CHAPTER 6
FORM 3: LAST WILL AND TESTAMENT (NO GUARDIANS)

FORM 3 IS A WILL WITH NO GUARDIANS PARAGRAPH

Form 3 is just like the Will in Form 2 and is flexible and lets people gift their property most ways. But Form 3 unlike Form 2 has no "Guardians" paragraph and is a Will for a person without a child under 18 and not giving anything to any minors under 18.

THIS BOOK'S 3 WILL FORMS SHOULD HELP MOST WITHOUT ANY CHANGES

As explained in this book a "Will" is a common document done by a person to control issues that may arise after their death. This book's forms show with blank spaces and underlining where most words, signatures, and dates should be added. This book's writing does show ways to add legal language or modify words in forms, but changing forms is rarely needed and can by risky to do.

WILL IN FORM 3 HAS BASIC LAYOUT WITH SEVERAL PARTS

The Will in Form 3 has a basic layout. Right at its start there is a place for the person making the Will to write their full legal name and last county of residence in Michigan.

The 1st paragraph, "Gifts", has many spaces to make either specific gifts of particular property or to make gifts of money amounts.

The 2nd paragraph, "Tangible Personal Property List", says to follow any such lists people ever do.

The 3rd paragraph, "Residue", has a "residue" clause to give anything not given by other parts of the Will or in other ways to whoever is named here (many people use this to give most things).

The 4th paragraph, "Administration", has space to name a person as "executor" (also called "personal representative") to handle some matters after someone's death.

This Will in Form 3 has no "Guardians" paragraph.

The 5th paragraph, "Miscellaneous", is made up of many sentences of legal language written to help avoid certain legal problems and to explain the Will.

Last in the form is a place for the person doing the Will to sign, and a place for 2 witnesses to sign.

35

RESIDUE CLAUSE HAS 2 PLACES TO NAME PERSONS TO GET THINGS

In a Will's "residue clause" anything not given by other parts of the Will or other means is gifted to the persons named in the clause. A residue clause is a "catch-all" making sure all property and money goes to someone. Many people use a residue clause to gift most their things since this is easy, avoids having to describe property, and has less legal risk. This Will's residue clause is written to have:

1) a 1st space to name 1 or more persons to get the residue (but any named here must survive to get things or their share goes to others named here), and

2) a 2nd space to name people to get things if all in the 1st space don't survive (any named here who don't survive have their share go to descendants and not others named here).

Most people name in the 1st space a spouse or closest family, and in the 2nd space most people name their next closest family or friends. Very helpful options exist to use with the residue clause:

a) People can in the residue clause leave the 1st space empty and only name people in the 2nd space to ensure if someone named dies their descendants get their share;

b) People can repeat names in the 2 clause spaces if there is only 1 person or group to target;

c) People can in either of the residue clause's spaces gift by percentages.

This residue clause may seem complex but usually whoever is named in the 1st used space gets things if they are living when the Will maker dies.

WILL IS DONE BY TESTATOR AND 2 WITNESSES COMPLETING PARAGRAPHS

Wills are completed by the person doing the Will (called the "Testator") signing a "Testator" paragraph in front of 2 witnesses, and then 2 witnesses signing a "Witnesses" paragraph and writing their addresses in front of each other and Testator. Full names should be used. Some people hold up their Will and say to witnesses things like, "This is the Will I want and want you to witness". In the paragraphs people sign a person can write in their own names and the date, or anyone can fill this in beforehand. Wills have some words about "perjury" and this book's Chapter 7 explains this. Most witnesses do not look at a Will except to read the paragraph they sign. Witnesses can be family, getting Will gifts, or the executor or guardian or conservator, but it is best if witnesses are not connected in these ways. Witnesses must be over 18, but if possible not too old. All who sign should see the other's hands as they sign using a permanent pen or marker. To fight forgery or help with proof some people modify Wills to have spots to initial each page or have more than 2 witnesses.

36

FORM 3:
LAST WILL AND TESTAMENT (NO GUARDIANS)

LAST WILL AND TESTAMENT

I, _____ a resident of _____ County, Michigan, hereby make, publish, and declare this as my Last Will and Testament (called here my "Will"), and I hereby revoke any Wills and Codicils earlier made by me.

1. GIFTS. I give the following gifts which are specific gifts except any gifts of money amounts are general gifts:

I give _____ to _____ if they survive me;

I give _____ to _____ if they survive me;

I give _____ to _____ if they survive me;

I give _____ to _____ if they survive me;

I give _____ to _____ if they survive me;

I give _____ to _____ if they survive me;

I give _____ to _____ if they survive me;

I give _____ to _____ if they survive me;

I give _____ to _____ if they survive me;

and I give _____ to _____ if they survive me.

2. TANGIBLE PERSONAL PROPERTY LIST. If a list or written statement signed or handwritten by me gives tangible personal property as allowed by law including Michigan law at MCL 700.2513 then I make such gifts. All such writing are intended to be and are to be construed as part of one document to all be followed. If any property is given in multiple writings the page that appears most recently completed controls. But any such writings not found by 60 days after my death and the gifts in such writings shall abate and have no effect.

3. RESIDUE. I give all property not given or used by other Will provisions, and the rest, residue, and remainder of my estate, whether now owned or later acquired, wherever located, and of any kind and nature including personal, real, and mixed property, including all property which I die possessed or am in any way entitled (all of which is called the "residue" in this Will), as follows: to _____ if they survive me, but if they all do not survive me then I give the just described property to _____ or their lineal descendants per stirpes.

4. ADMINISTRATION. I name and appoint _____ as personal representative of my Will and my estate, also called "executor" in this Will.

5. MISCELLANEOUS. The following applies to this Will and generally.

I direct unsupervised administration of my estate and Will or less burdensome options.

Plural, singular, or gender meanings do not limit Will provisions, including use of "they".

Any personal representative, guardian of any type, and conservator serving under this Will or otherwise shall serve without bond, surety, or other security.

A gift shall be sold unless all beneficiaries getting a gift agree on how to use or sell a gift.

If a beneficiary does not survive then their share goes to any other beneficiaries of the gift in proportion to the share they are getting, including the residue and if a gift says survival is required and despite anti-lapse or similar laws, but not if an alternate beneficiary is provided.

No unfilled Will part or blank is a mistake or incomplete, including for the residue.

Priority of Will gifts of the same type is based on the order they appear in this Will.

"Give" and "gift" means the same as devise, bequest, grant, legacy or similar.

"Survive" or "surviving" means to not stop living before 60 days after my death, and if in a gift is an absolute condition that must be met and anti-lapse or similar laws have no effect.

In addition to powers given by MCL 700.3715, any personal representative, guardian, and conservator is given as much power, authority, and discretion that may be given by law, including power to do any acts any personal representative finds may be helpful.

Any personal representative shall have power to with no liability for change in value lease, assign, sell at public or private sale with or without public notice, mortgage, hold, invest, abandon, encumber, exchange, manage, operate, and transfer in any way any property including of the estate, settle claims for and against the estate or any person, and have power of sale over real property, all with no need for involvement or permission or act of a court or other party at any time, and all with no need for any filing or inventory or other thing.

Any personal representative has power to at any time pay debts of any amount of mine or my estate that they in their sole and absolute discretion find valid and timely and fair, like debts of a last illness or funeral or burial, with no inventory or filing or any court action.

Any personal representative has power to petition for, appoint a fiduciary for, or pay for ancillary estate action, transact with my estate or any trust without act of any person or court, give different kinds, portions or undivided interests in property to beneficiaries and assign value to all things, and do any distribution or division of my estate or property in cash or in kind.

For gifts or property going to a minor any personal representative without act of a court has power to choose to and make transfers to: the minor, conservator named by Will or court, or custodian under the Michigan Uniform Transfers to Minors Act or other law. Persons named conservator in this Will are hereby nominated custodian for such minors under the Michigan Uniform Transfers to Minors Act, or a personal representative may appoint a custodian.

Failure to make gifts to some family including children is intentional and not a mistake.

The residue includes lapsed or failed gifts, insurance paid to the estate, and property a testator had a power of appointment or testamentary disposition over.

TESTATOR

I, who am named _____, the Testator, sign my name to this document on _____, 20__, and I declare under penalty for perjury under the law of the state of Michigan that the following statements are true: this document is my Will; I sign it willingly; I sign it as my voluntary act for the purposes expressed in it; I am at least 18 years old, have sufficient mental capacity to make this Will, and am under no constraint or undue influence.

_____
Testator

WITNESSES

We, who are named _____ and _____, the Witnesses, sign our names to this document on _____, 20__, and we declare under penalty for perjury under the law of the state of Michigan that the following statements are true: the person signing this document as the Testator signs the document as his or her Will, signs it willingly, and executes it as his or her voluntary act for the purposes expressed in this Will; each of us in the Testator's presence signs this Will as witness to the Testator's signing; and to the best of our knowledge the Testator is at least 18 years old, has sufficient mental capacity to make this Will, and is under no constraint or undue influence.

_____   _____
Witness   Address

_____   _____
Witness   Address

CHAPTER 7
FORM 4: SELF-PROVING AFFIDAVIT

FORM 4 IS DONE WITH A WILL TO AVOID SOME LATER WORK

Form 4 is the "Self-Proving Affidavit" form which is a standard form by the legislature found in law at MCL 700.2504. This form reduces later legal work and makes the Will more likely to be followed, and this form can be used with any of the Wills in Form 1, Form 2, or Form 3 in this book.

DOING SELF-PROVING AFFIDAVIT WITH WILL IS OPTION TO REDUCE WORK

This form is optional but is often done when a Will is signed or anytime later to help with legal work done after the person who made the Will dies. If this form is not done witnesses to a Will signing may have to be found after a death and testify convincingly in court that the Will was signed correctly (or in some cases other evidence can be used). With this form it is more likely a Will can be sufficiently proven so is followed. Usually a Self-Proving Affidavit form is done minutes after a Will is signed, or the form can be done anytime later when people are before a notary. Although rare to make later supporting a Will easier some people modify a Will to have more than the normal 2 witnesses.

AFFIDAVIT IS DONE BY PERSON AND 2 WITNESSES SIGNING BEFORE NOTARY

To be valid the Self-Proving Affidavit form must be signed before a notary by the person who made the Will and 2 witnesses to Will signing. The form refers to "testator and the witnesses, respectively", and "respectively" just means to print in order first testator (the person doing the Will) then witnesses. The form in this book can be done anytime after a Will has been signed, but in Michigan law there is a more detailed form only good right when a Will is signed. A notary (or a "notary public") can be found at banks, insurance agencies, courthouses, or (often best to avoid delay and bother) by hiring a notary from the phonebook. When the form is completed it is usually kept by paperclip to the Will it supports.

SIGNING UNDER "PENALTY OF PERJURY" CAN ALSO SELF-PROVE WILL

Michigan law says a Will maker and 2 witnesses signing "under penalty of perjury" can self-prove a Will even with no notary. Due to this many Wills have a dozen words about perjury in Testator and witness paragraphs, and the Wills in Form 2 and Form 3 in this book have this. No action or trouble comes from having this language, and a Will often uses easy "to the best of our knowledge" wording so more people will sign. For people worried the words on perjury can be cut from paragraphs and a Will will still be valid. <u>But Self-Proving Affidavits are still used since they take little time, and judges prefer Self-Proving Affidavits and despite the law judges usually require more evidence if they are not done.</u>

FORM 4:
SELF-PROVING AFFIDAVIT

SELF-PROVING AFFIDAVIT

(MCL 700.2504)

The State of _____

County of _____

We, _____, _____, and _____, the testator and the witnesses, respectively, whose names are signed to the attached will, sign this document and have taken an oath, administered by the officer whose signature and seal appear on this document, to swear that all of the following statements are true: the individual signing this document as the will's testator executed the will as his or her will, signed it willingly or willingly directed another to sign for him or her, and executed it as his or her voluntary act for the purposes expressed in the will; each witness, in the testator's presence, signed the will as witness to the testator's signing; and, to the best of the witnesses' knowledge, the testator, at the time of the will's execution, was 18 years of age or older, was under no constraint or undue influence, and had sufficient mental capacity to make this will.

_____

(Signature) Testator

_____

(Signature) Witness

_____

(Signature) Witness

Sworn to and signed in my presence by _____, the testator, and sworn to and signed in my presence by _____ and _____, witnesses, on _____, 20____.

month/day year

(SEAL)   Signed _____

_____

(official capacity of officer)

CHAPTER 8
FORM 5: TANGIBLE PERSONAL PROPERTY LIST

FORM 5 LETS GIFTS OF NORMAL PROPERTY BE WRITTEN OUTSIDE A WILL

Form 5 is the "Tangible Personal Property List" form written to comply with Michigan law, and it lets people write in a list gifts of tangible personal property to occur on a person's death.

FORM LETS PEOPLE WRITE IN SIMPLE LISTS WANTED GIFTS

Michigan law to make things easier lets people write anytime a list of gifts of tangible personal property to occur on a person's death. Michigan law at MCL 700.2513 says in part,

> "[A] will may refer to a written statement or list to dispose of items of tangible personal property not otherwise specifically disposed of by the will, other than money[.]"

A list can be done or changed anytime before or after a Will, but a Will must authorize lists. To cancel a list it can be destroyed, marked "void" or "canceled", or thrown away. To avoid some legal problems this book's list form and most the Wills require a person to get a gift survive by 60 days and says lists not found within 60 days of death have no effect. This book's list form and most Wills let several lists be done, but to avoid problems it is better to do 1 big list all stapled together and signed on 1 day.

LIST ONLY GIVES "TANGIBLE PERSONAL PROPERTY" NOT IN WILL

A list gives only "tangible" property so things with tangible form (not accounts or most investments), only "personal" property so things other than real property (not land or buildings), and not money (so no coins or paper money even if antiques or in a collection). Property used in a trade or business usually should not be given in a list but in a Will somehow. Usually lists are used to gift furniture, appliances, clothing, tools, collectibles, vehicles, and jewelry. Improper items written in a list will be ignored. And a list can only give property not specifically given in a Will, so a Will specific gift will be followed over a gift in a list. To be valid a list gift must describe items and persons with "reasonable certainty". Examples of gifts in a list are: "1998 Ford truck to Joe Blunt", "6 inch Saw to Ivy Smith", "All Fishing Equipment to Joy Fox", "Irish Cups to Jen and Kim Coe", "1.1 ct diamond ring to Kim Plum".

TANGIBLE PERSONAL PROPERTY LIST JUST MUST BE SIGNED AND DATED

To be valid a Tangible Personal Property List form just must be signed and there is also a place for a date. A list fully in a person's handwriting is valid too. To be followed lists must be found after a person's death, and lists are often kept paperclipped to a Will or nearby.

FORM 5:
TANGIBLE PERSONAL PROPERTY LIST

TANGIBLE PERSONAL PROPERTY LIST

I, the undersigned, wish this to be a list referred to by Will that gives tangible personal property as allowed by law including Michigan law at MCL 700.2513.
I understand only tangible personal property can be given and only things not specifically disposed of by Will. I give the items of property listed below to the beneficiary named next to the items but only if the beneficiary survives me by 60 days. This list and gifts in it have no effect if not found by 60 days after my death.

PROPERTY ITEMS   **NAMES OF BENEFICIARIES**

_____   _____

_____   _____

_____   _____

_____   _____

_____   _____

_____   _____

_____   _____

_____   _____

_____   _____

_____   _____

_____   _____

_____   _____

_____   _____

DATE: _____   SIGNED:_____

CHAPTER 9
FORM 6: CODICIL

FORM 6 "CODICIL" FORM CAN BE USED TO CHANGE PARTS OF A WILL

To change parts of an existing Will it is better to do a new Will to reduce the chance of confusion about what words are meant. But if wanted one can use a "Codicil" to change parts of a Will.

IN CODICIL TO CHANGE WILL JUST LIST WORDS TO REMOVE AND TO ADD

In a Codicil form usually one first writes the words to be removed from a Will, then one writes the new words to be added to a Will. Normally one also writes the date of the Will being modified. Often these removals and additions are simple things, for example replacing a beneficiary name, replacing property in a gift, adding a new gift, deleting a gift, or naming a different person as executor, guardian, or conservator. These things might be done because people named in a Will have died or no longer need things, or because gifted property in a Will is no longer owned so needs to be replaced.

CODICIL MUST BE SIGNED BEFORE 2 WITNESSES WHO SIGN

To be valid a Codicil must be signed just like a Will and meet all the normal requirements for a Will signing. Basically, the person making the document must sign before 2 witnesses who also sign. When completed a Codicil document should be kept so it is found with the Will it modifies. If wanted a "Self-Proving Affidavit" can be done to make the later work of showing a Codicil was signed correctly easier, and a form for this is in Michigan law at MCL700.2504(3)

FORM 6:
CODICIL

CODICIL

I, _____, a resident of _____ County, Michigan, declare this to be a Codicil to my Will dated _____.

FIRST: I hereby do revoke the part of my Will that reads as follows:

_____

_____

_____ .

SECOND: I hereby do add the following part to my Will:

_____

_____

_____ .

THIRD: In all other respects I hereby do confirm and republish the above-described Will.

TESTATOR

I, the Testator, sign, publish, and declare that I sign and execute this instrument as my Codicil, that I sign it willingly as a free and voluntary act for the purposes expressed therein, and that I am at least 18 years of age and of sound mind and under no constraint or undue influence, this __ day of _____, 20__.

_____
Testator

WITNESSES

We, the undersigned, declare and certify that in our presence the foregoing instrument was willingly published, declared, and signed by the above-named Testator as his or her Codicil, that to the best of our knowledge the Testator is at least 18 years of age and of sound mind and under no constraint or undue influence, that each of us is at least 18 years old, and that in the presence and hearing of Testator and each other we hereby sign our names as witnesses.

_____   _____
Witness   Address

_____   _____
Witness   Address

CHAPTER 10
FORM 7: DURABLE POWER OF ATTORNEY FOR HEALTH CARE

FORM LETS PERSON NAME PATIENT ADVOCATE AND GIVE INSTRUCTIONS

This form lets people name a "Patient Advocate" to help control health care, and if wanted give health care orders. This book's form is the form some agencies use. Some call this an "Advance Directive" or "Living Will" (the name of an older form).

CAN NAME SOMEONE "PATIENT ADVOCATE" IN CASE EVER INCAPACITATED

In a form someone at least 18 can be named "Patient Advocate" to control health care if 2 doctors find a person is incapacitated and can't control things due to lack of consciousness, communication, or concentration. The law usually gives power to (in order) a spouse, child, parents, and other family, but naming a person in a form can save time and costs. A Patient Advocate must serve "best interests" of a person, but above all must follow all written or verbal orders. A Patient Advocate or family in charge may see medical records. A Patient Advocate usually is given the signed form to show to others.

FORM CAN HAVE LIFE-SUSTAINING, ORGAN DONATION, AND OTHER ORDERS

In the form a person can give health care instructions. The "Life Sustaining Treatment" part of the form can give a Patient Advocate power to a) withhold care that may allow death, b) do a Do-Not-Resuscitate, and c) decide on forced feeding and water. A Patient Advocate can't act in ways that may shorten life unless power is clearly given by filling out areas on the form. Next, the "Organ Donation" part of the form can give the Patient Advocate power over organ donation. Lastly, the "Statement of Wishes" part of the form can have a person either a) not state any wishes, or b) they can write health care "wishes" that a Patient Advocate and doctors must follow. Most people fill out the form to give a Patient Advocate a lot of power but don't write many instructions since they trust them to act wisely. Hospitals and similar usually follow a form but usually doctors are also talked to and other forms done.

DO FORM BY PERSON SIGNING BEFORE 2 WITNESSES WHO ALSO SIGN

The form to be valid must be signed with 2 witnesses who must be at least 18 and not close family, not employees of a health care or insurance company involved, not likely to financially benefit like from a Will gift, and not named Patient Advocate in the form. The person named Patient Advocate later signs the last form page, the "Acceptance" page. Revocation of a form is done by telling or writing this to the Patient Advocate or others, and then doctors and others giving care should be told.

50

FORM 7:
DURABLE POWER OF ATTORNEY FOR HEALTH CARE

DURABLE POWER OF ATTORNEY FOR HEALTH CARE

I, _____ (print or type your full name), living at
_____ (print or type your
address), and being of sound mind, voluntarily choose a Patient Advocate to make care, custody, and medical treatment decisions for me.

This durable power of attorney for health care is only effective when I am unable to make my own medical decisions.

I may change my mind at any time by communicating in any manner that this designation does not reflect my wishes.

APPOINTMENT OF PATIENT ADVOCATE

I designate the person named below to be my Patient Advocate.

Name _____
Relationship _____
Address_____
Phone Number _____

If that person cannot serve I designate the person named below as Alternate Patient Advocate.

Name _____
Relationship _____
Address_____
Phone Number _____

My patient advocate or successor patient advocate must sign an acceptance before he or she can act. I have discussed this appointment with the persons I designated.

GENERAL POWERS

My patient advocate or successor patient advocate shall have power to make care, custody and medical treatment decisions for me if my attending physician and another physician or licensed psychologist determine I am unable to participate in medical treatment decisions.
My patient advocate has authority to consent to or refuse treatment on my behalf, to arrange medical and personal services for me, including admission to a hospital or nursing care facility, and to pay for such services with my funds.

My patient advocate shall have access to any of my medical records to which I have a right, immediately upon signing an Acceptance. This shall serve as a release under the Health Insurance Portability and Accountability Act.

Immediately upon signing an Acceptance, my patient advocate shall have access to my birth certificate and other legal documents needed to apply for Medicare, Medicaid, and other government programs.

POWER REGARDING LIFE-SUSTAINING TREATMENT (OPTIONAL)

I expressly authorize my patient advocate to make decisions to withhold or withdraw treatment which would allow me to die, and I acknowledge such decisions could or would allow my death. My patient advocate can sign a do-not-resuscitate declaration for me. My patient advocate can refuse food and water administered to me through tubes.

_____

(Sign your name if you wish to give your patient advocate this authority)

POWER REGARDING ORGAN DONATION (OPTIONAL)

I expressly authorize my patient advocate to make a gift any needed organs or body parts for the purposes of transplantation, therapy, medical research or education. The gift is effective upon my death. Unlike other powers I give to my patient advocate, this power remains after my death.

_____

(Sign your name if you wish to give your patient advocate this authority)

STATEMENT OF WISHES

My patient advocate has authority to make decisions in a wide variety of circumstances. In this document, I can express general wishes regarding conditions, specify particular types of treatment I do or do not want, or I may state no wishes at all. **CHOOSE A OR B.**

A.   I choose not to express any wishes in this document. This choice shall not be interpreted as limiting the power of my patient advocate to make any particular decision in any particular circumstance.

- OR -

B.   My wishes are as follows (you may attach more sheets of paper):

_____

_____

_____

_____

_____

_____

_____

_____

_____

LIABILITY

It is my intent no one involved in my care shall be liable for honoring my wishes as expressed in this designation or for following the directions of my patient advocate. Photocopies of this document can be relied upon as if they were originals.

SIGNATURE

I sign this document voluntarily, and I understand its purpose.

Dated: _____ Signed:_____
(Your signature)

_____
(Address)

STATEMENT REGARDING WITNESSES

I have chosen two adult witnesses who are not named in my will; who are not my spouse, parent, child, grandchild, brother or sister; who are not my physician or my patient advocate; who are not an employee of my life or health insurance company, an employee of a home for the aged where I reside, an employee of community mental health program providing me services or an employee at the health care facility where I am now.

STATEMENT AND SIGNATURE OF WITNESSES

We sign below as witnesses. This declaration was signed in our presence. The declarant appears to be of sound mind, and to be making this designation voluntarily, without duress, fraud or undue influence.

_____   _____
(Print name)   (Signature of witness)

_____
(Address)

_____   _____
(Print name)   (Signature of witness)

_____
(Address)

ACCEPTANCE BY PATIENT ADVOCATE

(1) This designation shall not become effective unless the patient is unable to participate in decisions regarding the patient's medical or mental health, as applicable. If this patient advocate designation includes the authority to make an anatomical gift as described in section 5506, the authority remains exercisable after the patient's death.

(2) A patient advocate shall not exercise powers concerning the patient's care, custody and medical or mental health treatment that the patient, if the patient were able to participate in the decision, could not have exercised in his or her own behalf.

(3) This designation cannot be used to make a medical treatment decision to withhold or withdraw treatment from a pregnant patient that would result in the pregnant patient's death.

(4) A patient advocate may make a decision to withhold or withdraw treatment which would allow a patient to die only if the patient has expressed in a clear and convincing manner that the patient advocate is authorized to make such a decision, and that the patient acknowledges that such a decision could or would allow the patient's death.

(5) A patient advocate shall not receive compensation for the performance of his or her authority, rights, and responsibilities, but a patient advocate may be reimbursed for actual and necessary expenses incurred in the performance of his or her authority, rights, and responsibilities.

(6) A patient advocate shall act in accordance with the standards of care applicable to fiduciaries when acting for the patient and shall act consistent with the patient's best interests. The known desires of the patient expressed or evidenced while the patient is able to participate in medical or mental heath treatment decisions are presumed to be in the patient's best interests.

(7) A patient may revoke his or her designation at any time or in any manner sufficient to communicate an intent to revoke.

(8) A patient may waive his or her right to revoke the patient advocate designation as to the power to make mental health treatment decisions, and if such waiver is made, his or her ability to revoke as to certain treatment will be delayed for 30 days after the patient communicates his or her intent to revoke.

(9) A patient advocate may revoke his or her acceptance to the designation at any time and in any manner sufficient to communicate an intent to revoke.

(10) A patient admitted to a health facility or agency has the rights enumerated in Section 20201 of the Public Health Code, Act No. 368 of the Public Acts of 1978, Being Section 333.20201 of the Michigan Compiled Laws.

I, _____, understand the above
               (Name of patient advocate)
conditions and I accept the designation as patient advocate or successor patient advocate for

_____.
              (Name of patient)

Dated: _____

Signed: _____
          (Signature of patient advocate or successor patient advocate)

CHAPTER 11
FORM 8: DO-NOT-RESUSCITATE ORDER

FORM 8 LETS ONE SAY NOT TO TRY RESTART HEART OR BREATHING

Form 8 is the "Do-Not-Resuscitate Order" form often called a "D.N.R.". This book's form is the standard form written by the Michigan legislature and found in law at MCL 333.1054. The forms lets people order no attempts to restart a heart or breathing should be be tried by paramedics or others.

FORM ORDERS NOT TO ATTEMPT TO RESTART HEART OR BREATHING

People in extreme bad health can ask for a Do-Not Resuscitate Order, and a person's doctors usually provides the form and explains it. The main part of the form simply says, "in the event my heart and breathing should stop [...] no person shall attempt to resuscitate me". The form is usually used by people at home or when traveling. The form is not used in hospitals, nursing homes, or similar places where instead doctors talk to patients to learn their wishes and other forms are done. Paramedics and other in a hurry usually only look for and follow a Do-Not-Resuscitate Order, and not other forms. Michigan after 2016 may start the similar "Provider Orders for Scope of Treatment" form too.

KEEP FORM NEAR BODY TO BE FOLLOWED BUT IT CAN BE REVOKED

To make sure a form is seen by paramedics or others to be followed people should keep it near or on their body, or wear a special "bracelet" showing form details. But a person not incapacitated is free to verbally or in writing revoke a form (like ask for C.P.R. from paramedics). After revocation all who saw a form should be told or they may continue to follow the form.

FORM IS COMPLETED BY PERSON, 2 WITNESSES, AND DOCTOR SIGNING

To be valid a Do-Not-Resuscitate Order is signed by a doctor, by 2 witnesses who witness the signing, and by either a person for themselves (they are called the "Declarant" in the form), or by a Patient Advocate, or by a Guardian. These other persons only have power if a person cannot control their own care, and they can only do a Do-Not-Resuscitate Order form if this matches a person's instructions and known beliefs. The 2 witnesses who witness the signing and then sign too must be at least 18 and at least 1 witness cannot be a spouse, parent, child, grandchild, brother or sister, or person likely to inherit. There is another Do-Not-Resuscitate Order form in the law for use by people who for religious reasons don't use doctors.

56

FORM 8:
DO-NOT-RESUSCITATE ORDER

DO-NOT-RESUSCITATE ORDER

This do-not-resuscitate order is issued by _____, attending
physician for _____.
(Type or print declarant's or ward's name)

Use the appropriate consent section below, A or B or C.

A. DECLARANT CONSENT

I have discussed my health status with my physician named above. I request that in the event my heart and breathing should stop, no person shall attempt to resuscitate me. This order will remain in effect until it is revoked as provided by law. Being of sound mind, I voluntarily execute this order, and I understand its full import.

_____   _____
(Declarant's signature)   (Date)

_____   _____
(Signature of person who signed for   (Date)
declarant, if applicable)

_____
(Type or print full name)

B. PATIENT ADVOCATE CONSENT

I authorize that in the event the declarant's heart and breathing should stop, no person shall attempt to resuscitate the declarant. I understand the full import of this order and assume responsibility for its execution. This order will remain in effect until it is revoked as provided by law.

_____   _____
(Patient advocate's signature)   (Date)

_____
(Type or print patient advocate's name)

C. GUARDIAN CONSENT

I authorize that in the event the ward's heart and breathing should stop, no person shall attempt to resuscitate the ward. I understand the full import of this order and assume responsibility for its execution. This order will remain in effect until it is revoked as provided by law.

_____   _____
(Guardian's signature)   (Date)

_____
(Type or print guardian's name)

_____   _____
(Physician's signature)   (Date)

_____
(Type or print physician's full name)

ATTESTATION OF WITNESSES

The individual who has executed this order appears to be of sound mind, and under no duress, fraud, or undue influence. Upon executing this order, the declarant (has) (has not) received an identification bracelet.

_____   _____
(Witness signature)   (Date)   (Witness signature)   (Date)

_____   _____
(Type or print witness's name)   (Type or print witness's name)

THIS FORM WAS PREPARED PURSUANT TO,
AND IS IN COMPLIANCE WITH,
THE MICHIGAN DO-NOT-RESUSCITATE PROCEDURE ACT.

CHAPTER 12
FORM 9: DURABLE GENERAL POWER OF ATTORNEY

FORM 9 LETS PERSON GIVE POWER TO ACT TO SOMEONE

Form 9 lets a person give power to someone to act for them (usually a spouse, other relative, or trusted friend and rarely an attorney), and often this is called a "Financial Power of Attorney".

FORM GIVES POWER TO SOMEONE TO LET THEM HELP BY DOING THINGS

The Durable General Power of Attorney form lets a person (the "Principal") give power to someone to act for them (the "Attorney-in-Fact"). Often given power is a spouse or friend to let them pay bills, use accounts, sell property, and see records when a person is sick, away, or busy. Using this form may avoid a court guardianship or nursing home. After a form is done a person still has power to do things and can overrule the Attorney-in-Fact. A form is revoked by a writing to an Attorney-in-Fact, and others who saw the form should be told to stop them relying on the form. When a form is being used others should be told and it should shown by signatures, like "Joy Wu as Attorney-in-Fact for Ed Wu".

FORM IS DURABLE AND GENERAL BUT OTHER OPTIONS ARE NOT USED

This book's form is "Durable" since it can be used even if a person is incapacitated, but power ends on death. The form is "General" since it gives broad power, but some special powers are not given including health care. The form is valid when signed and is not a "springing" form effective on an event. Some forms have "successor agents" or "coagents" but this can have legal problems.

FORM IS DANGEROUS AND POWER-OF-ATTORNEY HAS LEGAL DUTIES

This form is rarely used in part because it lets the Attorney-in-Fact do dangerous things like sell a principal's property, use accounts, borrow money, and sign binding contracts. An Attorney-in-Fact has a legal duty to act in "best interests" of the principal and follow instructions and keep records, but misconduct may not be seen until too late. It is usually improper to use a form to gift away a principal's money or property or take unusual actions at all and if this may occur a lawyer is needed.

FORM SIGNED BEFORE NOTARY AND LATER ACKNOWLEDGMENT IS SIGNED

It is standard for the form to be signed by a person before 2 witnesses and a notary. Witnesses should not be named Attorney-in-Fact in the forms. Later the person given power in the form signs the last page, the "Acknowledgment" page. The signed form is usually given to the person given power, but sometimes it is kept for safety by a person or their spouse and only given out when needed.

FORM 9:
DURABLE GENERAL POWER OF ATTORNEY

DURABLE GENERAL POWER OF ATTORNEY

ARTICLE 1 – APPOINTMENT OF ATTORNEY-IN-FACT

1.1 I, _____ , residing at _____ ,
make this Power of Attorney as the Principal and do hereby appoint as my Attorney-in-Fact
_____ residing at _____ ,
with the power to act as authorized by this instrument.

ARTICLE 2 – IMMEDIATELY EFFECTIVE AND DURABLE

2.1 This Power of Attorney is immediately effective from the date it is executed until my death unless I revoke it while competent as provided in this document.

2.2 This Power of Attorney is a durable Power of Attorney including under MCL 700.5501. This Power of Attorney is not affected by the principal's subsequent disability or incapacity, or by the lapse of time. This Power of Attorney is not affected by uncertainty over if I am alive.

ARTICLE 3 – GENERAL POWER OF ATTORNEY

3.1 My Attorney-in-Fact shall have all the powers incident to a general Power of Attorney under the common law and laws of Michigan, and shall have power and authority to act or do any thing as I could do if personally present, and shall also have full authority to take any actions necessary or incident to the execution of these powers.

ARTICLE 4 – LIMITATION ON POWERS

4.1 Limit Relating to Attorney-in-Fact's Estate. The powers given to my Attorney-in-Fact in this instrument shall be construed and limited so that no assets of my estate will be included in the estate of my Attorney-in-Fact if my Attorney-in-Fact predeceases me.

4.2 Limit Relating to Insurance. This instrument shall not be construed to grant my Attorney-in-Fact any incident of ownership in or powers over life insurance policies on my life.

4.3 Limit Relating to Will. My Attorney-in-Fact cannot sign a Will or Codicil on my behalf.

ARTICLE 5 – COMPENSATION TO ATTORNEY-IN-FACT

5. Payment to Attorney-in-Fact . My Attorney-in-Fact shall be entitled to, and may take from any funds including from my estate, reasonable compensation for the services performed under this instrument and is entitled to reimbursement for all reasonable out-of-pocket expenses incurred on my behalf or for my benefit.

ARTICLE 6 – RELIANCE BY OTHERS

6. Reliance By Others. All persons dealing with my Attorney-in-Fact may rely on a photocopy of this document. Revocation is not effective until third parties get actual notice. I agree to indemnify and hold harmless any party for claims related to reliance on this document.

ARTICLE 7 – RECORDS

7. Records. My Attorney-in-Fact shall keep reasonable records of transactions and acts done on my behalf and shall render reports and accounts as required by law or whenever I request.

ARTICLE 8 – GOVERNED UNDER MICHIGAN LAW

8. Governing Law. This instrument shall be governed by the laws of the State of Michigan in all respects including its validity, construction, interpretation and termination as a durable general Power of Attorney. If any provision is determined to be invalid, such invalidity shall not affect the validity of any other provisions.

<u>SIGNATURE OF PRINCIPAL</u>

_____   _____
Signature of Principal   Date

_____
Printed name of Principal

<u>STATEMENT OF WITNESSES AND SIGNATURES</u>

We, the undersigned witnesses who are at least 18 years old and not named Attorney-in-Fact in this document, do hereby say this document was signed in the presence of both of us by the above-named principal who appeared to be at least 18 years old and of sound mind and under no constraint or undue influence.

Witness:_____   Witness:_____

<u>NOTARY</u>

Acknowledged before me in _____ County, Michigan, on _____, by
_____, the above-named Principal.

Notary Stamp: Notary Signature:

               _____

ACKNOWLEDGMENT BY ATTORNEY-IN-FACT

I, _____, have been appointed as attorney-in-fact for _____, the principal, under a durable power of attorney dated _____. By signing this document, I acknowledge that if and when I act as attorney-in-fact, all of the following apply:

(a) Except as provided in the durable power of attorney, I must act in accordance with the standards of care applicable to fiduciaries acting under durable powers of attorney.

(b) I must take reasonable steps to follow the instructions of the principal.

(c) Upon request of the principal, I must keep the principal informed of my actions. I must provide an accounting to the principal upon request of the principal, to a guardian or conservator appointed on behalf of the principal upon the request of that guardian or conservator, or pursuant to judicial order.

(d) I cannot make a gift from the principal's property, unless provided for in the durable power of attorney or by judicial order.

(e) Unless provided in the durable power of attorney or by judicial order, I, while acting as attorney-in-fact, shall not create an account or other asset in joint tenancy between the principal and me.

(f) I must maintain records of my transactions as attorney-in-fact, including receipts, disbursements, and investments.

(g) I may be liable for any damage or loss to the principal, and may be subject to any other available remedy, for breach of fiduciary duty owed to the principal. In the durable power of attorney, the principal may exonerate me of any liability to the principal for breach of fiduciary duty except for actions committed by me in bad faith or with reckless indifference. An exoneration clause is not enforceable if inserted as the result of my abuse of a fiduciary or confidential relationship to the principal.

(h) I may be subject to civil or criminal penalties if I violate my duties to the principal.

Signature: _____   Date: _____

CHAPTER 13
FORM 10: POWER OF ATTORNEY OVER CHILD

FORM 10 LETS SOMEONE BE GIVEN POWER OVER A CHILD

Form 10 is the "Power Of Attorney Over Child" form and it lets a parent share power over a child under 18 with someone they choose. If the parent who did the form dies the form has no more effect.

GIVING SOMEONE POWER OVER CHILD MAY BE HELPFUL

This form may help if a child under 18 is away from a parent for any period of time and with a relative, teacher, babysitter, or friend for any reason like camp, school, medical care, travel, vacation, or parent incarceration. The person given power in the form can do all a parent can do like consent to a child's medical care to avoid dangerous delays, control schooling, control schedule and activities, and control all home and discipline issues. Some schools require more before newly enrolling a child not living with a parent or legal guardian. Legally the form is a "Power of Attorney" form, and the person given power is called "Attorney-in-Fact" or "Agent". A "guardian" who is not a parent can also give power over a minor using this form if they make minor changes.

FORM VALID FOR 6 MONTHS BUT PARENT KEEPS POWER AND CAN REVOKE

By law the form is valid for up to 6 months, but the form can be redone repeatedly. A parent always keeps power and can overrule an Attorney-in-Fact and if wanted can reclaim a child. The form can be revoked by a writing saying it is revoked given to the Attorney-in-Fact, and then others who saw the form should be told or they may keep relying on the form. Children turning 18 often do a "Durable Power of Attorney for Health Care" to let parents if needed see records and help control health care.

FORM SIGNED BEFORE NOTARY AND LATER ACKNOWLEDGMENT IS SIGNED

In Michigan it is standard for the form to be signed by a person before 2 witnesses and a notary. Witnesses should not be named Attorney-in-Fact in the form. The form requires 1 parent sign but people can modify the form to have 2 parents sign which is recommended to give the form more authority. Later the person given power in the form signs the last page, the "Acknowledgment" page. The form once signed usually is given to the person given power, and schools and doctors and others usually are shown copies of the form.

FORM 10:
POWER OF ATTORNEY OVER CHILD

POWER OF ATTORNEY OVER CHILD

I, _____, am a parent of the person now under 18 years of age named _____ who was born on _____ (who is called in the remainder of this document "the child").

I hereby make this Power of Attorney as the Principal and appoint as my Attorney-in-Fact _____ with the power to act as authorized by this instrument.

Pursuant to Michigan law MCL 700.5103 and other law I give my Attorney-in-Fact all powers and authority as parent regarding the care, custody, property, and all other matters involving the child which can be given or are delegable, including power to control, request, and consent to:

transport to or admission to a hospital or any other facility,

medical and surgical and dental treatment,

drugs and medications and scans and tests of any kind and nature for any reason,

medical or other records or information of the child including if confidential or privileged,

insurance and other benefits including from a government for the child,

schedule, discipline, household, food, clothing, and related matters,

money and property due to the child or owned by the child including taking possession, and

education and any activities for the child.

No power over marriage or adoption is given.

The document is effective immediately when signed and shall be effective for 6 months.

Revocation is not effective until third parties get actual notice, and I agree to indemnify any party for claims related to reliance on this document.

Copies of this document are as valid as the original and may be relied upon.

This Power of Attorney is not affected by the principal's subsequent disability or incapacity, or by the lapse of time. This document is not affected by uncertainty over if principal is alive.

SIGNATURE

Signed:_____   Dated:_____

NOTARY

Acknowledged before me in _____ County, Michigan, on _____,

by _____.

Notary Stamp: Notary Signature: _____

WITNESS SIGNATURES

Witness: _____   Witness: _____

ACKNOWLEDGMENT BY ATTORNEY-IN-FACT
(for Power Of Attorney Over Child)

I, _____, have been appointed as attorney-in-fact for _____, the principal, under a durable power of attorney dated _____. By signing this document, I acknowledge that if and when I act as attorney-in-fact, all of the following apply:

(a) Except as provided in the durable power of attorney, I must act in accordance with the standards of care applicable to fiduciaries acting under durable powers of attorney.

(b) I must take reasonable steps to follow the instructions of the principal.

(c) Upon request of the principal, I must keep the principal informed of my actions. I must provide an accounting to the principal upon request of the principal, to a guardian or conservator appointed on behalf of the principal upon the request of that guardian or conservator, or pursuant to judicial order.

(d) I cannot make a gift from the principal's property, unless provided for in the durable power of attorney or by judicial order.

(e) Unless provided in the durable power of attorney or by judicial order, I, while acting as attorney-in-fact, shall not create an account or other asset in joint tenancy between the principal and me.

(f) I must maintain records of my transactions as attorney-in-fact, including receipts, disbursements, and investments.

(g) I may be liable for any damage or loss to the principal, and may be subject to any other available remedy, for breach of fiduciary duty owed to the principal. In the durable power of attorney, the principal may exonerate me of any liability to the principal for breach of fiduciary duty except for actions committed by me in bad faith or with reckless indifference. An exoneration clause is not enforceable if inserted as the result of my abuse of a fiduciary or confidential relationship to the principal.

(h) I may be subject to civil or criminal penalties if I violate my duties to the principal.

Signature: _____   Date: _____

APPENDIX A:
HOW TO DOWNLOAD LEGAL FORMS

TO GET FORMS PEOPLE CAN (1) DOWNLOAD FORMS FREE AS EXPLAINED ON THIS PAGE, OR (2) PHOTOCOPY BOOK PAGES.

BOOK BUYERS ARE AUTHORIZED TO DOWNLOAD AND COPY FORMS FOR THEIR OWN AND THEIR FAMILY'S USE.

FILES TO DOWNLOAD ARE IN BOTH:

1) <u>PDF</u> FORMAT WHERE NO CHANGES CAN BE MADE BUT IT CAN BE PRINTED, AND

2) <u>WORD</u> FORMAT WHERE CHANGES CAN BE MADE BY TYPING IN WORDS AND IT CAN BE PRINTED.

<u>DOWNLOAD FORMS AT THESE LINKS:</u>

ge.tt/23IJyJC2

ge.tt/1Lqh0KC2

app.box.com/s/gifd9nlaxozm34d5nc9xz1uoqawf1qyx

mediafire.com/folder/6ipmcdy0h1f2b/mi

mediafire.com/view/z4p8dqjps45b1yc/miforms.pdf

mediafire.com/view/530t655p2m9kqwr/miforms.doc

4shared.com/folder/6lhINH7_/mi_online.html

EMAIL ANY COMMENTS TO <u>DAVENPORTPRESS@GMAIL.COM</u> .

APPENDIX B: SAMPLE FILLED OUT LEGAL FORMS

The rest of this book has sample filled out legal forms including sample Wills.

All forms in this book can be filled out by pen or marker (and most people do this), and using a computer or typewriter to neatly complete forms is not legally required.

All signatures and dates by signatures should be handwritten with permanent pen or marker and not done by a computer or typewriter.

People need not worry about neatness or small mistakes since a document is usually fine if those people who knew a decedent in life can tell the likely meaning.

For forms with blank lines people can type or handwrite words into these however wanted, and can:
    1) type in (or handwrite) words into a line ("I appoint ___John Doe____ as Agent"),
    2) use underlining so added words look underlined, maybe using whited out commas to hold underlining ("I appoint __John Doe__ as Agent"), or
    3) remove blank lines so it looks like normal text ("I appoint John Doe as Agent"), but removing lines can make added words hard to see so some people put added words in bold ("I appoint **John Doe** as Agent").

SAMPLE FILLED OUT LEGAL FORMS

SAMPLE FILLED OUT
FORM 1:
MICHIGAN STATUTORY WILL

MICHIGAN STATUTORY WILL NOTICE

1. An individual age 18 or older and of sound mind may sign a will.

2. There are several kinds of wills. If you choose to complete this form, you will have a Michigan statutory will. If this will does not meet your wishes in any way, you should talk with a lawyer before choosing a Michigan statutory will.

3. Warning! It is strongly recommended that you do not add or cross out any words on this form except for filling in the blanks because all or part of this will may not be valid if you do so.

4. This will has no effect on jointly held assets, on retirement plan benefits, or on life insurance on your life if you have named a beneficiary who survives you.

5. This will is not designed to reduce estate taxes.

6. This will treats adopted children and children born outside of wedlock who would inherit if their parent died without a will the same way as children born or conceived during marriage.

7. You should keep this will in your safe deposit box or other safe place. By paying a small fee, you may file this will in your county's probate court for safekeeping. You should tell your family where the will is kept.

8. You may make and sign a new will at any time. If you marry or divorce after you sign this will, you should make and sign a new will.

INSTRUCTIONS:

1. To have a Michigan statutory will, you must complete the blanks on the will form. You may do this yourself, or direct someone to do it for you. You must either sign the will or direct someone else to sign it in your name and in your presence.

2. Read the entire Michigan statutory will carefully before you begin filling in the blanks. If there is anything you do not understand, you should ask a lawyer to explain it to you.

MICHIGAN STATUTORY WILL OF __ROBERT KENNETH SWANSON__

(Print or type your full name)

ARTICLE 1. DECLARATIONS

This is my will and I revoke any prior wills and codicils.

I live in __Washtenaw__ County, Michigan.

My spouse is __Mary Katrina Swanson__

(Insert spouse's name or write "none")

My children now living are:

__Linda Rebecca Swanson__   __Timothy Oliver Swanson__

(Insert names or write "none")

ARTICLE 2. DISPOSITION OF MY ASSETS

2.1 CASH GIFTS TO PERSONS OR CHARITIES.

(Optional)

I can leave no more than two (2) cash gifts. I make the following cash gifts to the persons or charities in the amount stated here. Any transfer tax due upon my death shall be paid from the balance of my estate and not from these gifts.

Full name and address of person or charity to receive cash gift (name only 1 person or charity here):

__John Maxwell Swanson__

(Insert name of person or charity)

__88 Rockford Road, Ann Arbor, MI 48029__

(Insert address)

AMOUNT OF GIFT (In figures): $ __25,800__

AMOUNT OF GIFT (In words): __twenty-five thousand eight hundred__ Dollars

__*Robert Kenneth Swanson*__

(Your signature)

Full name and address of person or charity to receive cash gift (name only 1 person or charity here):

__Suzie Bette Winchester__

(Insert name of person or charity)

__792 23rd Street, Apartment # 392, Ann Arbor, MI 48029__

(Insert address)

AMOUNT OF GIFT (In figures): $ __7,821__

AMOUNT OF GIFT (In words): __seven thousand eight hundred twenty-one__ Dollars

__*Robert Kenneth Swanson*__

(Your signature)

74

2.2 PERSONAL AND HOUSEHOLD ITEMS.

I may leave a separate list or statement, either in my handwriting or signed by me at the end, regarding gifts of specific books, jewelry, clothing, automobiles, furniture, and other personal and household items.

I give my spouse all my books, jewelry, clothing, automobiles, furniture, and other personal and household items not included on such a separate list or statement. If I am not married at the time I sign this will or if my spouse dies before me, my personal representative shall distribute those items, as equally as possible, among my children who survive me. If no children survive me, these items shall be distributed as set forth in paragraph 2.3.

2.3 ALL OTHER ASSETS.

I give everything else I own to my spouse. If I am not married at the time I sign this will or if my spouse dies before me, I give these assets to my children and the descendants of any deceased child. If no spouse, children, or descendants of children survive me, I choose 1 of the following distribution clauses by signing my name on the line after that clause. If I sign on both lines, if I fail to sign on either line, or if I am not now married, these assets will go under distribution clause (b).

Distribution clause, if no spouse, children, or descendants of children survive me.

(Select only 1)

(a) One-half to be distributed to my heirs as if I did not have a will, and one-half to be distributed to my spouse's heirs as if my spouse had died just after me without a will.

_____

(Your signature)

(b) All to be distributed to my heirs as if I did not have a will.

_____*Robert Kenneth Swanson*_____

(Your signature)

ARTICLE 3. NOMINATIONS OF PERSONAL REPRESENTATIVE, GUARDIAN, AND CONSERVATOR

Personal representatives, guardians, and conservators have a great deal of responsibility. The role of a personal representative is to collect your assets, pay debts and taxes from those assets, and distribute the remaining assets as directed in the will. A guardian is a person who will look after the physical well-being of a child. A conservator is a person who will manage a child's assets and make payments from those assets for the child's benefit. Select them carefully. Also, before you select them, ask them whether they are willing and able to serve.

3.1 PERSONAL REPRESENTATIVE.

(Name at least 1)

I nominate _____Mary Katrina Swanson my wife_____ of

(Insert name of person or eligible financial institution)

__34 Main Street, Ann Arbor, MI 48029_____ to serve as personal representative.

(Insert address)

If my first choice does not serve, I nominate ____Millicent Kay Hutcher my sister_____

(Insert name of person or eligible financial institution)

of ___892 Pine Lane, Ann Arbor, MI 48032_____ to serve as personal representative.

(Insert address)

75

3.2 GUARDIAN AND CONSERVATOR.

Your spouse may die before you. Therefore, if you have a child under age 18, name an individual as guardian of the child, and an individual or eligible financial institution as conservator of the child's assets. The guardian and the conservator may, but need not be, the same person.

If a guardian or conservator is needed for a child of mine, I nominate

__Millicent Kay Hutcher my sister__ of __87 Deerfield Lane, Ann Arbor, MI 38021__
      (Insert name of individual)   (Insert address)

as guardian and   __Millicent Kay Hutcher my sister__
              (Insert name of individual or eligible financial institution)

of __87 Deerfield Lane, Ann Arbor, MI 38021__   to serve as conservator.
          (Insert address)

If my first choice cannot serve, I nominate _____
                                          (Insert name of individual)

of _____
                                 (Insert address)

as guardian and _____
              (Insert name of individual or eligible financial institution)

of _____ to serve as conservator.
         (Insert address)

3.3 BOND.

A bond is a form of insurance in case your personal representative or a conservator performs improperly and jeopardizes your assets. A bond is not required. You may choose whether you wish to require your personal representative and any conservator to serve with or without bond. Bond premiums would be paid out of your assets. (Select only 1)

(a) My personal representative and any conservator I have named shall serve with bond.

_____
(Your signature)

(b) My personal representative and any conservator I have named shall serve without bond.

_____ *Robert Kenneth Swanson* _____
(Your signature)

3.4 DEFINITIONS AND ADDITIONAL CLAUSES.

Definitions and additional clauses found at the end of this form are part of this will.

I sign my name to this Michigan statutory will on *July 7* 20 *15* .

_____ *Robert Kenneth Swanson* _____
(Your signature)

76

NOTICE REGARDING WITNESSES

You must use 2 adults who will not receive assets under this will as witnesses. It is preferable to have 3 adult witnesses. All the witnesses must observe you sign the will, have you tell them you signed the will, or have you tell them the will was signed at your direction in your presence.

STATEMENT OF WITNESSES

We sign below as witnesses, declaring that the individual who is making this will appears to be of sound mind and appears to be making this will freely, without duress, fraud, or undue influence, and that the individual making this will acknowledges that he or she has read the will, or has had it read to him or her, and understands the contents of this will.

__Douglas Eric Forrester__
(Print name)
__*Douglas Eric Forrester*__
(Signature of witness)
__87 Easy Street__
(Address)
__Golden Valley__   __MI__   __38092__
City)   (State)   (Zip)

__Evelyn Grace Forrester__
(Print name)
__*Evelyn Grace Forrester*__
(Signature of witness)
__87 Easy Street__
(Address)
__Golden Valley__   __MI__   __38092__
City)   (State)   (Zip)

_____
(Print name)

_____
(Signature of witness)

_____
(Address)

_____   _____   _____
(City)   (State)   (Zip)

DEFINITIONS

The following definitions & rules of construction apply to this Michigan statutory will:

(a) "Assets" means all types of property you can own, such as real estate, stocks and bonds, bank accounts, business interests, furniture, and automobiles.

(b) "Descendants" means your children, grandchildren, and their descendants.

(c) "Descendants" or "children" includes individuals born or conceived during marriage, individuals legally adopted, and individuals born out of wedlock who would inherit if their parent died without a will.

(d) "Jointly held assets" means those assets to which ownership is transferred automatically upon the death of 1 of the owners to the remaining owner or owners.

(e) "Spouse" means your husband or wife at the time you sign this will.

(f) Whenever a distribution under a Michigan statutory will is to be made to an individual's descendants, the assets are to be divided into as many equal shares as there are then living descendants of the nearest degree of living descendants and deceased descendants of that same degree who leave living descendants. Each living descendant of the nearest degree shall receive 1 share. The remaining shares, if any, are combined and then divided in the same manner among the surviving descendants of the deceased descendants as if the surviving descendants who were allocated a share and their surviving descendants had predeceased the descendant. In this manner, all descendants who are in the same generation will take an equal share.

(g) "Heirs" means those persons who would have received your assets if you had died without a will, domiciled in Michigan, under the laws that are then in effect.

(h) "Person" includes individuals and institutions.

(i) Plural and singular words include each other, where appropriate.

(j) If a Michigan statutory will states that a person shall perform an act, the person is required to perform that act. If a Michigan statutory will states that a person may do an act, the person's decision to do or not to do the act shall be made in good faith exercise of the person's powers.

ADDITIONAL CLAUSES
Powers of Personal Representative

1. A personal representative has all powers of administration given by Michigan law to personal representatives and, to the extent funds are not needed to meet debts and expenses currently payable and are not immediately distributable, the power to invest and reinvest the estate from time to time in accordance with the Michigan prudent investor rule. In dividing and distributing the estate, the personal representative may distribute partially or totally in kind, may determine the value of distributions in kind without reference to income tax bases, and may make non-pro rata distributions.

2. The personal representative may distribute estate assets otherwise distributable to a minor beneficiary to the minor's conservator or, in amounts not exceeding $5,000.00 per year, either to the minor, if married; to a parent or another adult with whom the minor resides and who has the care, custody, or control of the minor, or to the guardian. The personal representative is free of liability and is discharged from further accountability for distributing assets in compliance with the provisions of this paragraph.

POWERS OF GUARDIAN AND CONSERVATOR

A guardian named in this will has the same authority with respect to the child as a parent having legal custody would have. A conservator named in this will has all of the powers conferred by law.

SAMPLE FILLED OUT
FORM 2:
LAST WILL AND TESTAMENT (WITH GUARDIANS)

LAST WILL AND TESTAMENT

I, ___Henry James Ford___ a resident of ___Wayne___ County, Michigan, hereby make, publish, and declare this as my Last Will and Testament (called here my "Will"), and I hereby revoke any Wills and Codicils earlier made by me.

1. GIFTS. I give the following gifts which are specific gifts except any gifts of money amounts are general gifts:

I give ___1.5 carat diamond___ to ___Zelda Grace Jones___ if they survive me;

I give ___$125,000___ to ___John David Walker___ if they survive me;

I give ___63 Ivy Road, Lundy, Michigan, including land, buildings, and fixtures___ to ___Greta Olivia Parupski___ if they survive me;

I give ___$7,281.35___ to ___Wanda Kay Zinski___ if they survive me;

I give ___Irish engraved ring___ to ___Harriet Rush Smith___ if they survive me;

I give ___all jewelry not given above___ to ___Hannah Eve Pidoski___ if they survive me;

I give ___U.S. Bank savings account ending in #8923___ to ___John Hatcher my cousin___ if they survive me;

I give ___antique oak tables and chairs, grandfather clock, and all lamps___ to ___Anne Janet Lynn-Hutchinson___ if they survive me;

I give ___808 Lake Rd., Fish, Michigan, including land, buildings, and fixtures, and all property there not given above in this Will___ to ___Greg Frank Nox___ if they survive me;

I give ___1998 Ford truck___ to ___John Hatcher my cousin___ if they survive me; and

I give _____ to _____ if they survive me.

2. TANGIBLE PERSONAL PROPERTY LIST. If a list or written statement signed or handwritten by me gives tangible personal property as allowed by MCL 700.2513 or other law then I make such gifts. All such writings that are sufficient to give property are intended to be and are to be construed as part of one document to all be followed. If any property is given in multiple writings the page with the more recent date or attached to a page with a more recent date controls. Gifts in writings not found by 60 days after my death shall abate and have no effect.

3. RESIDUE. I give all my property remaining and not given or used by other Will provisions or other ways, whether now owned or later acquired, wherever located, and of any kind and nature including personal, real, and mixed property, including the rest, residue, and remainder of my estate (all of which is called the "residue" in this Will), as follows: to __Mary Jennifer Ford my wife__ if they survive me, but if they all do not survive me then I give the just described property to __Lucy Kay Boyd and Mark Paul Ford my children__ or their lineal descendants per stirpes.

4. ADMINISTRATION. I name and appoint __Mary Jennifer Ford my wife__ as personal representative of my Will and my estate, also called here my "executor".

5. GUARDIANS. If any of my children have not reached age 18 I name and appoint __Margaret Kim Windsor my sister__ to be guardian of such children including of their person. I also name and appoint __Margaret Kim Windsor__ to be conservator of the estate of such children and their property or any other persons under age 18 who receive or possess property.

6. MISCELLANEOUS. The following applies to this Will and generally.

Plural, singular, or gender meaning of words and phrases do not limit any Will provision, and "they" means one or several persons or entities.

I request unsupervised administration and informal probate of my Will and estate.

Any personal representative, guardian of any type, and conservator serving under this Will or otherwise shall serve without bond, surety, or other security.

A gift going to multiple beneficiaries shall be sold by the personal representative and the sale proceeds distributed unless beneficiaries agree on how to use or sell the gift.

If part of a gift fails due to a beneficiary not surviving their share goes to any other beneficiaries in proportion to their shares, including the residue and if a gift says survival is required and despite anti-lapse laws, but not if an alternate beneficiary is provided.

No unfilled Will part or blank is a mistake or incomplete, including in the residue.

Priority of Will gifts of the same type is based on the order they appear here.

"Give" and "gift" means the same as devise, bequest, grant, legacy or similar.

"Survive" or "surviving" means to not stop living before 60 days after my death, and if in a gift it is an absolute condition that must be met and anti-lapse laws have no effect.

Any personal representative, guardian of any type, and conservator is given as much power, authority, and discretion that may be given by law, including power to with no liability for change in value sell, lease, assign, mortgage, invest, exchange, and transfer in any way any property, settle claims for and against the estate or any person, and have power of sale over real property, all with no need for act of a court at any time, and all with no need for any filing or inventory or other thing.

Any personal representative may and has power to at any time pay debts of mine or my estate that the personal representative in his or her sole and absolute discretion finds are valid including timely and fair, including debts of a last illness or funeral or burial or any similar things, all with no limit on amount, no need for filing or inventory or similar, and no need for court action at any time.

For gifts or other property going to minors including any of their estate my personal representative without act of any court has power as he or she chooses to make transfers to: the minor, a conservator named by Will or a court, or a custodian under the Michigan Uniform Transfers to Minors Act or similar law.

The residue includes lapsed or failed gifts, insurance paid to the estate, and property testator had a power of appointment or testamentary disposition over.

Gifts or failure to make gifts to family are intentional and no mistake in these is made.

TESTATOR

I, who am named ____Henry James Ford____ , the Testator, sign my name to this document on __November 2__ , 20_15_ , and I declare under penalty for perjury under the law of the state of Michigan that the following statements are true: this document is my Will; I sign it willingly; I sign it as my voluntary act for the purposes expressed in it; I am at least 18 years old, have sufficient mental capacity to make this Will, and am under no constraint or undue influence.

Henry James Ford
Testator

WITNESSES

We, who are named___Amy Janet Windsor__ and _Brian Adam Smith____ , the Witnesses, sign our names to this document on _November 2_ , 20_15_ , and we declare under penalty for perjury under the law of the state of Michigan that the following statements are true: the person signing this document as the Testator signs the document as his or her Will, signs it willingly, and executes it as his or her voluntary act for the purposes expressed in this Will; each of us in the Testator's presence signs this Will as witness to the Testator's signing; and to the best of our knowledge the Testator is at least 18 years old, has sufficient mental capacity to make this Will, and is under no constraint or undue influence.

Amy Janet Windsor   ___87 Main Street, Battle Creek, MI 48203___
Witness   Address
Brian Adam Smith   ___6328 Forest Lane, Fridley, MI 48211___
Witness   Address

82

SAMPLE FILLED OUT
FORM 3:
LAST WILL AND TESTAMENT (NO GUARDIANS)

LAST WILL AND TESTAMENT

I, **Ruth Miranda Kent** a resident of **Washtenaw** County, Michigan, hereby make, publish, and declare this as my Last Will and Testament (called here my "Will"), and I hereby revoke any Wills and Codicils earlier made by me.

1. GIFTS. I give the following gifts which are specific gifts except any gifts of money amounts are general gifts:

I give a total of $100,000 to 50% to Abraham Daniel Walker, 40% to Amy Ann Hope, and 10% to Jennifer Kim Beaufort if they survive me;

I give $900 and my cat Bob to Wanda Gina Sorenson if she survives me;

I give 1987 Ford Truck and any other vehicles I own of any type to Reginald William Porter my nephew if they survive me;

I give $20,000 to Greg Paul Best but if they fail to survive me then to his wife Mary Gertrude Best;

I give $990 to each of my first cousins if they survive me;

I give $5,000 to St. Mary Angelica of the Cross which was my old church in New York City if they survive me;

I give $2,250 to St. Joseph's my church if they survive me;.

I give $300 to Timmy Hart my paperboy if they survive me;

I give $20,000 to Juanita Chuzappa my helper but if they fail to survive me then to Juanita's Chuzappa's children;

I give $10,000 to Marion Dexter my neighbor but if they fail to survive me then to her husband Arthur Dexter; and

I give $10,000 total to Janet Wilkins, Miranda Britom, Cindy Spagor, Diana Linda Craigtown, and Teresa Germann if they survive me.

2. TANGIBLE PERSONAL PROPERTY LIST. If a list or written statement signed or handwritten by me gives tangible personal property as allowed by MCL 700.2513 or other law then I make such gifts. All such writings that are sufficient to give property are intended to be and are to be construed as part of one document to all be followed. If any property is given in multiple writings the page with the more recent date or attached to a page with a more recent date controls. Gifts in writings not found by 60 days after my death shall abate and have no effect.

3. RESIDUE. I give all my property remaining and not given or used by other Will provisions or other ways, whether now owned or later acquired, wherever located, and of any kind and nature including personal, real, and mixed property, including the rest, residue, and remainder of my estate (all of which is called the "residue" in this Will), as follows: to **Wanda Kim Dallas my daughter** if they survive me, but if they all do not survive me then I give the just described property to **Beverly Carol Yancy and Paul Alan Kent my cousins** or their lineal descendants per stirpes.

4. ADMINISTRATION. I name and appoint **Wanda Kim Dallas my daughter** as personal representative of my Will and my estate, also called here my "executor".

5. MISCELLANEOUS. The following applies to this Will and generally.

Plural, singular, or gender meaning of words and phrases do not limit any Will provision, and "they" means one or several persons or entities.

I request unsupervised administration and informal probate of my Will and estate.

Any personal representative, guardian of any type, and conservator serving under this Will or otherwise shall serve without bond, surety, or other security.

A gift going to multiple beneficiaries shall be sold by the personal representative and the sale proceeds distributed unless beneficiaries agree on how to use or sell the gift.

If part of a gift fails due to a beneficiary not surviving their share goes to any other beneficiaries in proportion to their shares, including the residue and if a gift says survival is required and despite anti-lapse laws, but not if an alternate beneficiary is provided.

No unfilled Will part or blank is a mistake or incomplete, including in the residue.

Priority of Will gifts of the same type is based on the order they appear here.

"Give" and "gift" means the same as devise, bequest, grant, legacy or similar.

"Survive" or "surviving" means to not stop living before 60 days after my death, and if in a gift it is an absolute condition that must be met and anti-lapse laws have no effect.

Any personal representative, guardian of any type, and conservator is given as much power, authority, and discretion that may be given by law, including power to with no liability for change in value sell, lease, assign, mortgage, invest, exchange, and transfer in any way any property, settle claims for and against the estate or any person, and have power of sale over real property, all with no need for act of a court at any time, and all with no need for any filing or inventory or other thing.

Any personal representative may and has power to at any time pay debts of mine or my estate that the personal representative in his or her sole and absolute discretion finds are valid including timely and fair, including debts of a last illness or funeral or burial or any similar things, all with no limit on amount, no need for filing or inventory or similar, and no need for court action at any time.

For gifts or other property going to minors including any of their estate my personal representative without act of any court has power to distribute power as he finds best.

The residue includes lapsed or failed gifts, insurance paid to the estate, and property testator had a power of appointment or testamentary disposition over.

Gifts or failure to make gifts to family are intentional and no mistake in these is made.

TESTATOR

I, who am named __Ruth Miranda Kent__ , the Testator, sign my name to this document on __December 30__ , 20_15_ , and I declare under penalty for perjury under the law of the state of Michigan that the following statements are true: this document is my Will; I sign it willingly; I sign it as my voluntary act for the purposes expressed in it; I am at least 18 years old, have sufficient mental capacity to make this Will, and am under no constraint or undue influence.

__*Ruth Miranda Kent*__

Testator

WITNESSES

We, who are named__ Julie Ann Totter __ and__ Hector Juan Perez __ , the Witnesses, sign our names to this document on __December 30__ , 20_15_ , and we declare under penalty for perjury under the law of the state of Michigan that the following statements are true: the person signing this document as the Testator signs the document as his or her Will, signs it willingly, and executes it as his or her voluntary act for the purposes expressed in this Will; each of us in the Testator's presence signs this Will as witness to the Testator's signing; and to the best of our knowledge the Testator is at least 18 years old, has sufficient mental capacity to make this Will, and is under no constraint or undue influence.

__*Julie Ann Totter*__   __92 4th Street, St. Paul, MI 48707__
Witness   Address
__*Hector Juan Perez*__   __2038 Madison, WI 48923__
Witness   Address

86

ADDITIONAL (#2)
SAMPLE FILLED OUT
FORM 2:
LAST WILL AND TESTAMENT (WITH GUARDIANS)

LAST WILL AND TESTAMENT

I, __Paul Eric Windsor a/k/a Petey Windsor__ a resident of __Scott__ County, Michigan, hereby make, publish, and declare this as my Last Will and Testament (called here my "Will"), and I hereby revoke any Wills and Codicils earlier made by me.

1. GIFTS. I give the following gifts which are specific gifts except any gifts of money amounts are general gifts:

I give __$10,000__ to __the United States Cancer Society__ if they survive me.

I give __$5,000 in total__ to __my cousin Kent Coleman's children__ if they survive me.

I give __$6,000 in total__ to __my cousin Carol Brubaker's children__ if they survive me.

I give __$500 each__ to __each of my grandchildren__ if they survive me.

2. TANGIBLE PERSONAL PROPERTY LIST. If a list or written statement signed or handwritten by me gives tangible personal property as allowed by MCL 700.2513 or other law then I make such gifts. All such writings that are sufficient to give property are intended to be and are to be construed as part of one document to all be followed. If any property is given in multiple writings the page with the more recent date or attached to a page with a more recent date controls. Gifts in writings not found by 60 days after my death shall abate and have no effect.

3. RESIDUE. I give all my property remaining and not given or used by other Will provisions or other ways, whether now owned or later acquired, wherever located, and of any kind and nature including personal, real, and mixed property, including the rest, residue, and remainder of my estate (all of which is called the "residue" in this Will), as follows: to _____ if they survive me, but if they all do not survive me then I give the just described property to
_____ my children John Terry Windsor, Pamela Kay Smith, Martha Fiona Peterson, Greta Samantha Windsor-Somonis, Vernon Chester Windsor, and Mary Kay Windsor,
_____ and my loved cousin Beverly Hannah Carlson, _____
_____ and my great friend William Frank Sommenheim _____
or their lineal descendants per stirpes.

88

4. ADMINISTRATION. I name and appoint ___my son John Terry Windsor___ as personal representative of my Will and my estate, also called here my "executor".

5. GUARDIANS. If any of my children have not reached age 18 I name and appoint ___John Terry Windsor___ to be guardian of the person of such children. I also name and appoint ___John Terry Windsor___ to be conservator of the estate of such children and their property or any other persons under age 18 who receive or possess property.

6. MISCELLANEOUS. The following applies to this Will and generally.

Plural, singular, or gender meaning of words and phrases do not limit any Will provision, and "they" means one or several persons or entities.

I request unsupervised administration and informal probate of my Will and estate.

Any personal representative, guardian of any type, and conservator serving under this Will or otherwise shall serve without bond, surety, or other security.

A gift going to multiple beneficiaries shall be sold by the personal representative and the sale proceeds distributed unless beneficiaries agree on how to use or sell the gift.

If part of a gift fails due to a beneficiary not surviving their share goes to any other beneficiaries in proportion to their shares, including the residue and if a gift says survival is required and despite anti-lapse laws, but not if an alternate beneficiary is provided.

No unfilled Will part or blank is a mistake or incomplete, including in the residue.

Priority of Will gifts of the same type is based on the order they appear here.

"Give" and "gift" means the same as devise, bequest, grant, legacy or similar.

"Survive" or "surviving" means to not stop living before 60 days after my death, and if in a gift it is an absolute condition that must be met and anti-lapse laws have no effect.

Any personal representative, guardian of any type, and conservator is given as much power, authority, and discretion that may be given by law, including power to with no liability for change in value sell, lease, assign, mortgage, invest, exchange, and transfer in any way any property, settle claims for and against the estate or any person, and have power of sale over real property, all with no need for act of a court at any time, and all with no need for any filing or inventory or other thing.

Any personal representative may and has power to at any time pay debts of mine or my estate that the personal representative in his or her sole and absolute discretion finds are valid including timely and fair, including debts of a last illness or funeral or burial or any similar things, all with no limit on amount, no need for filing or inventory or similar, and no need for court action at any time.

For gifts or other property going to minors including any of their estate my personal representative without act of any court has power as he or she chooses to make transfers to: the minor, a conservator named by Will or a court, or a custodian under the Michigan Uniform Transfers to Minors Act or similar law. For minors getting gifts in this Will or other transfers the person named conservator in this Will is nominated and named as custodian under the Michigan Uniform Transfers to Minors Act or similar law, or if they fail to serve any personal representative may name a custodian.

The residue includes lapsed or failed gifts, insurance paid to the estate, and property testator had a power of appointment or testamentary disposition over.

Gifts or failure to make gifts to family are intentional and no mistake in these is made.

TESTATOR

I, who am named ____Paul Eric Windsor____ , the Testator, sign my name to this document on ____March 19__, 2015_, and I declare under penalty for perjury under the law of the state of Michigan that the following statements are true: this document is my Will; I sign it willingly; I sign it as my voluntary act for the purposes expressed in it; I am at least 18 years old, have sufficient mental capacity to make this Will, and am under no constraint or undue influence.

_____*Paul Eric Windsor*_____
Testator

WITNESSES

We, who are named____Olivia Joy Pawlenty__ and _Roy Felix Pawlenty__ , the Witnesses, sign our names to this document on____March 19__, 2015_ , and we declare under penalty for perjury under the law of the state of Michigan that the following statements are true: the person signing this document as the Testator signs the document as his or her Will, signs it willingly, and executes it as his or her voluntary act for the purposes expressed in this Will; each of us in the Testator's presence signs this Will as witness to the Testator's signing; and to the best of our knowledge the Testator is at least 18 years old, has sufficient mental capacity to make this Will, and is under no constraint or undue influence.

____*Olivia Joy Pawlenty*____   __87 Hastings Avenue, Belle Plaine, MI 48607__
Witness   Address

__*Roy Felix Pawlenty*__   __87 Hastings Avenue, Belle Plaine, MI 48607__
Witness   Address

ADDITIONAL (#2)
SAMPLE FILLED OUT
FORM 3:
LAST WILL AND TESTAMENT (NO GUARDIANS)

LAST WILL AND TESTAMENT

I, __David Roger Widowonski__ a resident of __Oakland__ County, Michigan, hereby make, publish, and declare this as my Last Will and Testament (called here my "Will"), and I hereby revoke any Wills and Codicils earlier made by me.

1. GIFTS. I give the following gifts which are specific gifts except any gifts of money amounts are general gifts:

I give __a total of $50,000__ to __Brian Oscar Peterson, Michael Paul Peterson, and Mary Rebecca Hart__ if they survive me.

I give __a total of $6,000__ to __Beth Tina Smith and Frank M. Smith__ if they survive me.

I give __$5,000__ to __Loretta Marsha Swit in the hope she will help her daughter Megan Kara Switt__ if they survive me.

I give __$3,000__ to __Loretta Marsha Switt__ if they survive me.

I give __Wells Fargo savings account ending in #8923__ to __Lawrence Deer__ if they survive me.

I give __$5,000__ to __Fishy Smith my fishing buddy__ if they survive me.

I give __$2,000__ to __Mary Nixon__ but is she does not survive me then to __Karen Kay Paulson__ .

I give __all cars and trucks I own at my death__ to __Victor Perez my mechanic__ if they survive me.

I give __$7,002.21__ to __Brenda Mary Hill but if she fails to survive me then to her brother William Matthew Hill__ .

2. TANGIBLE PERSONAL PROPERTY LIST. If a list or written statement signed or handwritten by me gives tangible personal property as allowed by MCL 700.2513 or other law then I make such gifts. All such writings that are sufficient to give property are intended to be and are to be construed as part of one document to all be followed. If any property is given in multiple writings the page with the more recent date or attached to a page with a more recent date controls. Gifts in writings not found by 60 days after my death shall abate and have no effect.

3. RESIDUE. I give all my property remaining and not given or used by other Will provisions or other ways, whether now owned or later acquired, wherever located, and of any kind and nature including personal, real, and mixed property, including the rest, residue, and remainder of my estate (all of which is called the "residue" in this Will), as follows: to _____ if they survive me, but if they all do not survive me then I give the just described property to
<u>20% to Hector Samuel Widowonski, 30% to Kenneth Paul Widowonski, and</u>
<u>50% to Mary Janet Maxwell</u> or their lineal descendants per stirpes.

4. ADMINISTRATION. I name and appoint <u>Hector Samuel Widowonski</u> as personal representative of my Will and my estate, also called here my "executor".

5. MISCELLANEOUS. The following applies to this Will and generally.

Plural, singular, or gender meaning of words and phrases do not limit any Will provision, and "they" means one or several persons or entities.

I request unsupervised administration and informal probate of my Will and estate.

Any personal representative, guardian of any type, and conservator serving under this Will or otherwise shall serve without bond, surety, or other security.

A gift going to multiple beneficiaries shall be sold by the personal representative and the sale proceeds distributed unless beneficiaries agree on how to use or sell the gift.

If part of a gift fails due to a beneficiary not surviving their share goes to any other beneficiaries in proportion to their shares, including the residue and if a gift says survival is required and despite anti-lapse laws, but not if an alternate beneficiary is provided.

No unfilled Will part or blank is a mistake or incomplete, including in the residue.

Priority of Will gifts of the same type is based on the order they appear here.

"Give" and "gift" means the same as devise, bequest, grant, legacy or similar.

"Survive" or "surviving" means to not stop living before 60 days after my death, and if in a gift it is an absolute condition that must be met and anti-lapse laws have no effect.

Any personal representative, guardian of any type, and conservator is given as much power, authority, and discretion that may be given by law, including power to with no liability for change in value sell, lease, assign, mortgage, invest, exchange, and transfer in any way any property, settle claims for and against the estate or any person, and have power of sale over real property, all with no need for act of a court at any time, and all with no need for any filing or inventory or other thing.

Any personal representative may and has power to at any time pay debts of mine or my estate that the personal representative in his or her sole and absolute discretion finds are valid including timely and fair, including debts of a last illness or funeral or burial or any similar things, all with no limit on amount, no need for filing or inventory or similar, and no need for court action at any time.

For gifts or other property going to minors including any of their estate my personal representative without act of any court has power as he or she chooses to make transfers to: the minor, a conservator named by Will or a court, or a custodian under the Michigan Uniform Transfers to Minors Act or similar law. For minors getting gifts in this Will or other transfers the person named conservator in this Will is nominated and named as custodian under the Michigan Uniform Transfers to Minors Act or similar law, or if they fail to serve any personal representative may name a custodian.

The residue includes lapsed or failed gifts, insurance paid to the estate, and property testator had a power of appointment or testamentary disposition over.

Gifts or failure to make gifts to family are intentional and no mistake in these is made.

TESTATOR

I, who am named David Roger Widowonski , the Testator, sign my name to this document on July 5 , 2015 , and I declare under penalty for perjury under the law of the state of Michigan that the following statements are true: this document is my Will; I sign it willingly; I sign it as my voluntary act for the purposes expressed in it; I am at least 18 years old, have sufficient mental capacity to make this Will, and am under no constraint or undue influence.

David Roger Widowonski
Testator

WITNESSES

We, who are named Michael Frank Bjerk and Brian Douglas Thorpe , the Witnesses, sign our names to this document on July 5 , 2015 , and we declare under penalty for perjury under the law of the state of Michigan that the following statements are true: the person signing this document as the Testator signs the document as his or her Will, signs it willingly, and executes it as his or her voluntary act for the purposes expressed in this Will; each of us in the Testator's presence signs this Will as witness to the Testator's signing; and to the best of our knowledge the Testator is at least 18 years old, has sufficient mental capacity to make this Will, and is under no constraint or undue influence.

Michael Frank Bjerk   87 Main Street, Lansing, Michigan 48607
Witness   Address

Brian Douglas Thorpe   8 Hubert Street, Bloomington, Michigan 48609
Witness   Address

SAMPLE FILLED OUT
FORM 4:
SELF-PROVING AFFIDAVIT

SELF-PROVING AFFIDAVIT
(MCL 700.2504)

The State of __MICHIGAN__

County of __WASHTENAW__

We, __John Henry Tescatone__, __Mary Jennifer Bolger__, and __Karen Gina Kellogg__, the testator and the witnesses, respectively, whose names are signed to the attached will, sign this document and have taken an oath, administered by the officer whose signature and seal appear on this document, to swear that all of the following statements are true: the individual signing this document as the will's testator executed the will as his or her will, signed it willingly or willingly directed another to sign for him or her, and executed it as his or her voluntary act for the purposes expressed in the will; each witness, in the testator's presence, signed the will as witness to the testator's signing; and, to the best of the witnesses' knowledge, the testator, at the time of the will's execution, was 18 years of age or older, was under no constraint or undue influence, and had sufficient mental capacity to make this will.

John Henry Tescatone
(Signature) Testator

Mary Jennifer Bolger
(Signature) Witness

Karen Gina Kellogg
(Signature) Witness

Sworn to and signed in my presence by __John Henry Tescatone__, the testator, and sworn to and signed in my presence by __Mary Jennifer Bolger__ and __Karen Gina Kellogg__, witnesses, on __January 18__, 20 _16_.
                                                                    month/day year

Natalie Regina Notario

(SEAL)   Signed
                  __NOTARY__
                  (official capacity of officer)

96

SAMPLE FILLED OUT
FORM 5:
TANGIBLE PERSONAL PROPERTY LIST

TANGIBLE PERSONAL PROPERTY LIST

I, the undersigned, wish this to be a list referred to by Will that gives tangible personal property as allowed by law including Michigan law at MCL 700.2513.
I understand only tangible personal property can be given and only things not specifically disposed of by Will. I give the items of property listed below to the beneficiary named next to it but only if the beneficiary survives me by 60 days. This list has no effect if not found by 60 days after my death.

PROPERTY ITEMS	NAMES OF BENEFICIARIES
1998 Ford Truck	Samantha Bell
1.3 carat diamond ring	Abigail Sue Reed
Italian silver jewelry	Samantha Bell
14 ft power boat and kayak with paddles	Luke Mark Wheeler
Parkhurst-style bench	Rebecca Stewart
glass table and its wood chairs	Rebecca Stewart
set of 18 silver candlesticks	Mary and Cindy Lott
my wedding dress and shoes	Mary Lott
chainsaw with serial no. 382937	Larry Kelly
chainsaw with serial no. 89930484421	Brian Kelly
antique lanterns and repair kits for them	Jason Brooks
Tucker my pet dog and all his supplies	Susan Ditcher
oak lamp usually kept on porch	Susan Ditcher
all sewing machines and fabrics	Mary Kay Poppler
rocking chair bought in Oregon	Robert Schmidt
all fishing poles and fishing equipment	Elwood Blues
coin collection in 8 glass cases	Millard Filmore

DATE: __May 2, 2016__   SIGNED: *John William Filmore*

98

SAMPLE FILLED OUT
FORM 6:
CODICIL

CODICIL

I, __Jennifer Kay Polka__ , a resident of __Oakland__ County, Michigan, declare this to be a Codicil to my Will dated __March 2, 2015_.

FIRST: I hereby do revoke the part of my Will that reads as follows:
_____I give $20,000 to Paul Jacob Farmer if they survive me_____

_____

_____I give my 1967 Corvette to Ned Baker_____.

SECOND: I hereby do add the following part to my Will:
_____I give $20,000 to Eve Susan Farmer if they survive me_____

_____.

THIRD: In all other respects I hereby confirm and republish the above-described Will.

TESTATOR

I, the Testator, sign, publish, and declare I sign and execute this instrument as my Codicil, that I sign it willingly as a free and voluntary act for the purposes expressed therein, and that I am at least 18 years of age and of sound mind and under no constraint or undue influence, this __8th__ day of __April__ , 20 _15_ .

_____*Jennifer Kay Polka*_____
Testator

WITNESSES

We, the undersigned, declare in our presence the foregoing instrument was willingly published, declared, and signed by the above-named Testator as his or her Codicil, that to the best of our knowledge the Testator is at least 18 years of age and of sound mind and under no constraint or undue influence, that each of us is at least 18 years old, and that in the presence and hearing of Testator and each other we hereby sign our names as witnesses.

__*Susan Vera Chomsky*__   __88 Hunter Street, Silver Bay, MI 48612__
Witness   Address

__*Norman Paul Chomsky*__   __88 Hunter Street, Silver Bay, MI 48612__
Witness   Address

SAMPLE FILLED OUT
FORM 7:
DURABLE POWER OF ATTORNEY FOR HEALTH CARE

DURABLE POWER OF ATTORNEY FOR HEALTH CARE

I, ___John David Smith___ (print or type your full name), living at
___465 Main Street, Ann Arbor, MI 48209___ (print or type your address),
and being of sound mind, voluntarily choose a Patient Advocate to make care, custody, and medical treatment decisions for me.

This durable power of attorney for health care is only effective when I am unable to make my own medical decisions.

I may change my mind at any time by communicating in any manner that this designation does not reflect my wishes.

APPOINTMENT OF PATIENT ADVOCATE

I designate the person named below to be my Patient Advocate.

Name ___Mary Jennifer Smith___
Relationship ___Wife___
Address ___465 Main Street, Ann Arbor, MI 48209___
Phone Number ___313-555-9382___

If that person cannot serve I designate the person named below as Alternate Patient Advocate.

Name _____
Relationship _____
Address _____
Phone Number _____

My patient advocate or successor patient advocate must sign an acceptance before he or she can act. I have discussed this appointment with the persons I designated.

GENERAL POWERS

My patient advocate or successor patient advocate shall have power to make care, custody and medical treatment decisions for me if my attending physician and another physician or licensed psychologist determine I am unable to participate in medical treatment decisions.
My patient advocate has authority to consent to or refuse treatment on my behalf, to arrange medical and personal services for me, including admission to a hospital or nursing care facility, and to pay for such services with my funds.

My patient advocate shall have access to any of my medical records to which I have a right, immediately upon signing an Acceptance. This shall serve as a release under the Health Insurance Portability and Accountability Act.

Immediately upon signing an Acceptance, my patient advocate shall have access to my birth certificate and other legal documents needed to apply for Medicare, Medicaid, and other government programs.

POWER REGARDING LIFE-SUSTAINING TREATMENT (OPTIONAL)

I expressly authorize my patient advocate to make decisions to withhold or withdraw treatment which would allow me to die, and I acknowledge such decisions could or would allow my death. My patient advocate can sign a do-not-resuscitate declaration for me. My patient advocate can refuse food and water administered to me through tubes.

John David Smith

(Sign your name if you wish to give your patient advocate this authority)

POWER REGARDING ORGAN DONATION (OPTIONAL)

I expressly authorize my patient advocate to make a gift any needed organs or body parts for the purposes of transplantation, therapy, medical research or education. The gift is effective upon my death. Unlike other powers I give to my patient advocate, this power remains after my death.

John David Smith

(Sign your name if you wish to give your patient advocate this authority)

STATEMENT OF WISHES

My patient advocate has authority to make decisions in a wide variety of circumstances. In this document, I can express general wishes regarding conditions, specify particular types of treatment I do or do not want, or I may state no wishes at all. **CHOOSE A OR B.**

A.   I choose not to express any wishes in this document. This choice shall not be interpreted as limiting the power of my patient advocate to make any particular decision in any particular circumstance.

- OR -

B.   My wishes are as follows (you may attach more sheets of paper):

_____

_____

I trust my Patient Advocate but if possible I want to stay near my home and would like Dr. John Kyle to be my doctor

_____

_____

_____

_____

103

LIABILITY

It is my intent no one involved in my care shall be liable for honoring my wishes as expressed in this designation or for following the directions of my patient advocate. Photocopies of this document can be relied upon as if they were originals.

SIGNATURE

I sign this document voluntarily, and I understand its purpose.

Dated: __March 19, 2016__   Signed: __John David Smith__
(Your signature)

__807 River Road, Grand Rapids, MI 48298__
(Address)

STATEMENT REGARDING WITNESSES

I have chosen two adult witnesses who are not named in my will; who are not my spouse, parent, child, grandchild, brother or sister; who are not my physician or my patient advocate; who are not an employee of my life or health insurance company, an employee of a home for the aged where I reside, an employee of community mental health program providing me services or an employee at the health care facility where I am now.

STATEMENT AND SIGNATURE OF WITNESSES

We sign below as witnesses. This declaration was signed in our presence. The declarant appears to be of sound mind, and to be making this designation voluntarily, without duress, fraud or undue influence.

__Eric Hector Hamilton__   __Eric Hector Hamilton__
(Print name)   (Signature of witness)

__7768 81st Street, Grand Rapids, MI 48297__
(Address)

__Janet Beverly Ford__   __Janet Beverly Ford__
(Print name)   (Signature of witness)

__887 River Road, Grand Rapids, MI 48298__
(Address)

ACCEPTANCE BY PATIENT ADVOCATE

(1) This designation shall not become effective unless the patient is unable to participate in decisions regarding the patient's medical or mental health, as applicable. If this patient advocate designation includes the authority to make an anatomical gift as described in section 5506, the authority remains exercisable after the patient's death.

(2) A patient advocate shall not exercise powers concerning the patient's care, custody and medical or mental health treatment that the patient, if the patient were able to participate in the decision, could not have exercised in his or her own behalf.

(3) This designation cannot be used to make a medical treatment decision to withhold or withdraw treatment from a pregnant patient that would result in the pregnant patient's death.

(4) A patient advocate may make a decision to withhold or withdraw treatment which would allow a patient to die only if the patient has expressed in a clear and convincing manner that the patient advocate is authorized to make such a decision, and that the patient acknowledges that such a decision could or would allow the patient's death.

(5) A patient advocate shall not receive compensation for the performance of his or her authority, rights, and responsibilities, but a patient advocate may be reimbursed for actual and necessary expenses incurred in the performance of his or her authority, rights, and responsibilities.

(6) A patient advocate shall act in accordance with the standards of care applicable to fiduciaries when acting for the patient and shall act consistent with the patient's best interests. The known desires of the patient expressed or evidenced while the patient is able to participate in medical or mental heath treatment decisions are presumed to be in the patient's best interests.

(7) A patient may revoke his or her designation at any time or in any manner sufficient to communicate an intent to revoke.

(8) A patient may waive his or her right to revoke the patient advocate designation as to the power to make mental health treatment decisions, and if such waiver is made, his or her ability to revoke as to certain treatment will be delayed for 30 days after the patient communicates his or her intent to revoke.

(9) A patient advocate may revoke his or her acceptance to the designation at any time and in any manner sufficient to communicate an intent to revoke.

(10) A patient admitted to a health facility or agency has the rights enumerated in Section 20201 of the Public Health Code, Act No. 368 of the Public Acts of 1978, Being Section 333.20201 of the Michigan Compiled Laws.

I, __Mary Jennifer Smith__ , understand the above
(Name of patient advocate)
conditions and I accept the designation as patient advocate or successor patient advocate for
__John David Smith__
(Name of patient)

Dated: __4-11-2016__

Signed: __*Mary Jennifer Smith*__
(Signature of patient advocate or successor patient advocate)

105

SAMPLE FILLED OUT
FORM 8:
DO-NOT-RESUSCITATE ORDER

DO-NOT-RESUSCITATE ORDER

This do-not-resuscitate order is issued by <u>Dr. Michael Jong Liu</u>, attending physician for <u>Brian Daniel Brubaker</u>.

(Type or print declarant's or ward's name)

Use the appropriate consent section below, A or B or C.

A. DECLARANT CONSENT

I have discussed my health status with my physician named above. I request that in the event my heart and breathing should stop, no person shall attempt to resuscitate me. This order will remain in effect until it is revoked as provided by law. Being of sound mind, I voluntarily execute this order, and I understand its full import.

<u>*Brian Daniel Brubaker*</u>   <u>8-22-2015</u>

(Declarant's signature)   (Date)

_____   _____

(Signature of person who signed for   (Date)
declarant, if applicable)

<u>Brian Daniel Brubaker</u>

(Type or print full name)

B. PATIENT ADVOCATE CONSENT

I authorize that in the event the declarant's heart and breathing should stop, no person shall attempt to resuscitate the declarant. I understand the full import of this order and assume responsibility for its execution. This order will remain in effect until it is revoked as provided by law.

_____   _____

(Patient advocate's signature)   (Date)

_____

(Type or print patient advocate's name)

107

C. GUARDIAN CONSENT

I authorize that in the event the ward's heart and breathing should stop, no person shall attempt to resuscitate the ward. I understand the full import of this order and assume responsibility for its execution. This order will remain in effect until it is revoked as provided by law.

_____   _____
(Guardian's signature)   (Date)

_____
(Type or print guardian's name)

_____*Michael Jong Liu*_____   _8-22-2015_
(Physician's signature)   (Date)

_____Dr. Michael Jong Liu_____
(Type or print physician's full name)

ATTESTATION OF WITNESSES

The individual who has executed this order appears to be of sound mind, and under no duress, fraud, or undue influence. Upon executing this order, the declarant (has) (has not) received an identification bracelet.

Geraldine Nina Bjerk 8-22-2015   *Charles Jon Windsor* 8-22-2015
(Witness signature)   (Date)   (Witness signature)   (Date)

_____Geraldine Nina Bjerk_____   _____Charles Jon Windsor_____
(Type or print witness's name)   (Type or print witness's name)

THIS FORM WAS PREPARED PURSUANT TO, AND IS IN COMPLIANCE WITH, THE MICHIGAN DO-NOT-RESUSCITATE PROCEDURE ACT.

SAMPLE FILLED OUT
FORM 9:
DURABLE GENERAL POWER OF ATTORNEY

DURABLE GENERAL POWER OF ATTORNEY

ARTICLE 1 – APPOINTMENT OF ATTORNEY-IN-FACT

1.1 I, __Adam Samuel Smith__ , residing at __101 Telegraph Hill, Pontiac, MI 48201__
make this Power of Attorney as the Principal and do hereby appoint as my Attorney-in-Fact
__Julie Karen Smith-Bextor__ , residing at __87 Broadway Street, Pontiac, MI 48201__
with the power to act as authorized by this instrument.

ARTICLE 2 – IMMEDIATELY EFFECTIVE AND DURABLE

2.1 This Power of Attorney is immediately effective from the date it is executed until my death unless I revoke it while competent as provided in this document.

2.2 This Power of Attorney is a durable Power of Attorney including under MCL 700.5501. This Power of Attorney is not affected by the principal's subsequent disability or incapacity, or by the lapse of time. This Power of Attorney is not affected by uncertainty over if I am alive.

ARTICLE 3 – GENERAL POWER OF ATTORNEY

3.1 My Attorney-in-Fact shall have all the powers incident to a general Power of Attorney under the common law and laws of Michigan, and shall have power and authority to act or do any thing as I could do if personally present, and shall also have full authority to take any actions necessary or incident to the execution of these powers.

ARTICLE 4 – LIMITATION ON POWERS

4.1 Limit Relating to Attorney-in-Fact's Estate. The powers given to my Attorney-in-Fact in this instrument shall be construed and limited so that no assets of my estate will be included in the estate of my Attorney-in-Fact if my Attorney-in-Fact predeceases me.

4.2 Limit Relating to Insurance. This instrument shall not be construed to grant my Attorney-in-Fact any incident of ownership in or powers over life insurance policies on my life.

4.3 Limit Relating to Will. My Attorney-in-Fact cannot sign a Will or Codicil on my behalf.

ARTICLE 5 – COMPENSATION TO ATTORNEY-IN-FACT

5. Payment to Attorney-in-Fact . My Attorney-in-Fact shall be entitled to, and may take from any funds including from my estate, reasonable compensation for the services performed under this instrument and is entitled to reimbursement for all reasonable out-of-pocket expenses incurred on my behalf or for my benefit.

ARTICLE 6 – RELIANCE BY OTHERS

6. Reliance By Others. All persons dealing with my Attorney-in-Fact may rely on a photocopy of this document. Revocation is not effective until third parties get actual notice. I agree to

indemnify and hold harmless any party for claims related to reliance on this document.

ARTICLE 7 – RECORDS

7. Records. My Attorney-in-Fact shall keep reasonable records of transactions and acts done on my behalf and shall render reports and accounts as required by law or whenever I request.

ARTICLE 8 – GOVERNED UNDER MICHIGAN LAW

8. Governing Law. This instrument shall be governed by the laws of the State of Michigan in all respects including its validity, construction, interpretation and termination as a general durable Power of Attorney. If any provision is determined to be invalid, such invalidity shall not affect the validity of any other provisions.

SIGNATURE OF PRINCIPAL

Adam Samuel Smith
Signature of Principal

12-15-2015
Date

Adam Samuel Smith
Printed name of Principal

STATEMENT AND SIGNATURES OF WITNESSES

We, the witnesses who sign immediately below are at least 18 years old and not named as Attorney-in-Fact in this document, and we do hereby say this document was signed in the presence of both of us by the above-named principal who appeared to be at least 18 years old and of sound mind and under no constraint or undue influence.

Witness: *Gertrude Amy Saxon*   Witness: *Mark Hugo Bayard*

NOTARY

Acknowledged before me in __Oakland__ County, Michigan, on __12-15-2015__ , by

__Adam Samuel Smith__ .

Notary Stamp: Notary Signature:

Natalie Ruth Notariolo

111

ACKNOWLEDGMENT BY ATTORNEY-IN-FACT

I, ___Julie Karen Smith-Bextor___ , have been appointed as attorney-in-fact for ___Adam Samuel Smith___ , the principal, under a durable power of attorney dated ___12-15-2015___ . By signing this document, I acknowledge that if and when I act as attorney-in-fact, all of the following apply:

(a) Except as provided in the durable power of attorney, I must act in accordance with the standards of care applicable to fiduciaries acting under durable powers of attorney.

(b) I must take reasonable steps to follow the instructions of the principal.

(c) Upon request of the principal, I must keep the principal informed of my actions. I must provide an accounting to the principal upon request of the principal, to a guardian or conservator appointed on behalf of the principal upon the request of that guardian or conservator, or pursuant to judicial order.

(d) I cannot make a gift from the principal's property, unless provided for in the durable power of attorney or by judicial order.

(e) Unless provided in the durable power of attorney or by judicial order, I, while acting as attorney-in-fact, shall not create an account or other asset in joint tenancy between the principal and me.

(f) I must maintain records of my transactions as attorney-in-fact, including receipts, disbursements, and investments.

(g) I may be liable for any damage or loss to the principal, and may be subject to any other available remedy, for breach of fiduciary duty owed to the principal. In the durable power of attorney, the principal may exonerate me of any liability to the principal for breach of fiduciary duty except for actions committed by me in bad faith or with reckless indifference. An exoneration clause is not enforceable if inserted as the result of my abuse of a fiduciary or confidential relationship to the principal.

(h) I may be subject to civil or criminal penalties if I violate my duties to the principal.

Signature: ___Julie Karen Smith-Bextor___ Date: ___12-15-2015___

112

SAMPLE FILLED OUT
FORM 10:
POWER OF ATTORNEY OVER CHILD

POWER OF ATTORNEY OVER CHILD

I, ___Pamela Mona Cunningham___ , am a parent of the person now under 18 years of age named <u>Bonita Kimberly Cunningham</u> who was born on ___Nov. 26, 2011___ (who is called in the remainder of this document "the child").

I hereby make this Power of Attorney as the Principal and do hereby appoint as my Attorney-in-Fact ___Marybeth Sue Kaiser___ with the power to act as authorized by this instrument.

I state that pursuant to Michigan law at MCL 700.5103 and other law I hereby delegate and give to my Attorney-in-Fact all my powers and authority as parent regarding the care, custody, and property of the child which are delegable or can be given, including power to:

control and consent to transport and also to admission at a hospital or other facility,
control and consent to medical and surgical and dental treatment,
control and consent to drugs and medications and also any scans or tests,
seek and review any medical or other records or information of the child,
control and seek insurance and benefits for the child,
control schedule, discipline, household, food, clothing, and related matters,
receive or control money and property due to the child or owned by the child, and
control and seek education and activities for the child.

No power over marriage or adoption is given.

The document is effective immediately when signed and shall be effective for 6 months.

Revocation is not effective until third parties get actual notice, and I agree to indemnify any party for claims related to reliance on this document.

Copies of this document are as valid as the original and may be relied upon.

This Power of Attorney is not affected by the principal's subsequent disability or incapacity, or by the lapse of time. This document is not affected by uncertainty over if principal is alive.

SIGNATURE

Signed: ___*Pamela Mona Cunningham*___   Dated: ___11-3-2015___

NOTARY

Acknowledged before me in __Wayne__ County, Michigan, on ___11-3-2015___, by ___Pamela Mona Cunningham___ .

Notary Stamp: Notary Signature:___*Nathan Juan Perez*___

WITNESS SIGNATURES

Witness: ___*Michael Larry Smith*___   Witness: ___*Harriet Lorna Doone*___

114

ACKNOWLEDGMENT BY ATTORNEY-IN-FACT

(for Power Of Attorney Over Child)

I, ___Marybeth Sue Kaiser___ , have been appointed as attorney-in-fact for Bonita Kimberly Cunningham_____ , the principal, under a durable power of attorney dated ___11-03-2015___ . By signing this document, I acknowledge that if and when I act as attorney-in-fact, all of the following apply:

(a) Except as provided in the durable power of attorney, I must act in accordance with the standards of care applicable to fiduciaries acting under durable powers of attorney.

(b) I must take reasonable steps to follow the instructions of the principal.

(c) Upon request of the principal, I must keep the principal informed of my actions. I must provide an accounting to the principal upon request of the principal, to a guardian or conservator appointed on behalf of the principal upon the request of that guardian or conservator, or pursuant to judicial order.

(d) I cannot make a gift from the principal's property, unless provided for in the durable power of attorney or by judicial order.

(e) Unless provided in the durable power of attorney or by judicial order, I, while acting as attorney-in-fact, shall not create an account or other asset in joint tenancy between the principal and me.

(f) I must maintain records of my transactions as attorney-in-fact, including receipts, disbursements, and investments.

(g) I may be liable for any damage or loss to the principal, and may be subject to any other available remedy, for breach of fiduciary duty owed to the principal. In the durable power of attorney, the principal may exonerate me of any liability to the principal for breach of fiduciary duty except for actions committed by me in bad faith or with reckless indifference. An exoneration clause is not enforceable if inserted as the result of my abuse of a fiduciary or confidential relationship to the principal.

(h) I may be subject to civil or criminal penalties if I violate my duties to the principal.

Signature: *Marybeth Sue Kaiser*   Date: ___11-03-2015___

115

END OF BOOK